Teen Alcoholism

Other Books of Related Interest:

Opposing Viewpoints Series

Alcohol

Teen Drug Abuse

Current Controversies

School Violence

Teen Pregnancy and Parenting

At Issue Series

Alcohol Abuse

Drunk Driving

CONTEMPORARY
ISSUES
COMPANION

Teen Alcoholism

Joseph Tardiff, Book Editor

GREENHAVEN PRESS
A part of Gale, Cengage Learning

GALE
CENGAGE Learning

Detroit • New York • San Francisco • New Haven, Conn • Waterville, Maine • London

Christine Nasso, *Publisher*
Elizabeth Des Chenes, *Managing Editor*

© 2008 Greenhaven Press, a part of Gale, Cengage Learning.

For more information, contact:
Greenhaven Press
27500 Drake Rd.
Farmington Hills, MI 48331-3535
Or you can visit our Internet site at gale.cengage.com

LIBRARY OF CONGRESS CATALOGING-IN-PUBLICATION DATA

Teen alcoholism / Joseph Tardiff, book editor.
    p. cm. -- (Contemporary issues companion)
    Includes bibliographical references and index.
    ISBN-13: 978-0-7377-3482-9 (hardcover)
    ISBN-10: 0-7377-3482-5 (hardcover)
    ISBN-13: 978-0-7377-3483-6 (pbk.)
    ISBN-10: 0-7377-3483-3 (pbk.)
    1. Teenagers--Alcohol use--United States--Juvenile literature. 2. Alcoholism--
United States--Juvenile literature. 3. Drinking of alocholic beverages--United
States--Juvenile literature. I. Tardiff, Joseph C., 1966-
    HV5135.T443 2008
    362.2920835'0973--dc22

                                                                    2007033053

Printed in the United States of America
   2 3 4 5 6   12 11 10 09 08

ED081

Contents

Foreword

In the news, on the streets, and in neighborhoods, individuals are confronted with a variety of social problems. Such problems may affect people directly: A young woman may struggle with depression, suspect a friend of having bulimia, or watch a loved one battle cancer. And even the issues that do not directly affect her private life—such as religious cults, domestic violence, or legalized gambling—still impact the larger society in which she lives. Discovering and analyzing the complexities of issues that encompass communal and societal realms as well as the world of personal experience is a valuable educational goal in the modern world.

Effectively addressing social problems requires familiarity with a constantly changing stream of data. Becoming well informed about today's controversies is an intricate process that often involves reading myriad primary and secondary sources, analyzing political debates, weighing various experts' opinions—even listening to firsthand accounts of those directly affected by the issue. For students and general observers, this can be a daunting task because of the sheer volume of information available in books, periodicals, on the evening news, and on the Internet. Researching the consequences of legalized gambling, for example, might entail sifting through congressional testimony on gambling's societal effects, examining private studies on Indian gaming, perusing numerous Web sites devoted to Internet betting, and reading essays written by lottery winners as well as interviews with recovering compulsive gamblers. Obtaining valuable information can be time-consuming—since it often requires researchers to pore over numerous documents and commentaries before discovering a source relevant to their particular investigation.

Greenhaven's Contemporary Issues Companion series seeks to assist this process of research by providing readers with useful and pertinent information about today's complex issues. Each volume in this anthology series focuses on a topic of current interest, presenting informative and thought-provoking selections written from a wide variety of viewpoints. The readings selected by the editors include such diverse sources as personal accounts and case studies, pertinent factual and statistical articles, and relevant commentaries and over views. This diversity of sources and views, found in every Contemporary Issues Companion, offers readers a broad perspective in one convenient volume.

In addition, each title in the Contemporary Issues Companion series is designed especially for young adults. The selections included in every volume are chosen for their accessibility and are expertly edited in consideration of both the reading and comprehension levels of the audience. The structure of the anthologies also enhances accessibility. An introductory essay places each issue in context and provides helpful facts such as historical background or current statistics and legislation that pertain to the topic. The chapters that follow organize the material and focus on specific aspects of the book's topic. Every essay is introduced by a brief summary of its main points and biographical information about the author. These summaries aid in comprehension and can also serve to direct readers to material of immediate interest and need. Finally, a comprehensive index allows readers to efficiently scan and locate content.

The Contemporary Issues Companion series is an ideal launching point for research on a particular topic. Each anthology in the series is composed of readings taken from an extensive gamut of resources, including periodicals, newspapers, books, government documents, the publications of private and public organizations, and Internet Web sites. In these volumes, readers will find factual support suitable for use in reports, debates, speeches, and research papers. The anthologies also facilitate further research, featuring a book and periodical bibliography and a list of organizations to contact for additional information.

A perfect resource for both students and the general reader, Greenhaven's Contemporary Issues Companion series is sure to be a valued source of current, readable information on social problems that interest young adults. It is the editors' hope that readers will find the Contemporary Issues Companion series useful as a starting point to formulate their own opinions about and answers to the complex issues of the present day.

Introduction

The United States is one of just four countries in the world—including Mongolia, Indonesia, and Palau—whose minimum legal drinking age is twenty-one. Yet many observers maintain that despite this restriction, teenage alcohol abuse in the United States has reached epidemic levels. A 2005 study conducted by the Substance Abuse and Mental Health Services Administration (SAMHSA) shows that about 10.8 million American youths aged twelve to twenty (28.2 percent of this age group) reported drinking alcohol in the past month. Nearly 7.2 million (18.8 percent) were binge drinkers (i.e., drinking at least five drinks at one time), and 2.3 million (6 percent) were heavy drinkers.[1] According to David Jernigan, research director for the Center on Alcohol Marketing and Youth (CAMY) at Georgetown University. "This is the nation's No. 1 drug problem—7,000 kids under the age of 16 start drinking every day."[2]

Government agencies, law enforcement officials, and alcohol prohibition groups have steadfastly maintained that a more rigorous enforcement of minimum-age laws at the state and local levels would significantly reduce the underage-drinking problem. Despite this, there has been a movement in recent years to roll back the minimum-age limit to eighteen or nineteen. The principal advocates of this stance are university administrators and educators who have witnessed first-hand the often appalling effects rampant alcohol abuse and binge drinking have on college campuses by underage students. According to university representatives, the longstanding policy of strict prohibition has not altered teenage attitudes toward drinking: rather, it has pushed the problem underground where it is more difficult to monitor. Prohibition is a failure, they argue, and it is time for parents and other adult authority figures to take a more progressive role in teaching teenagers how to drink alcohol responsibly.

The history of the current minimum-age law can be traced back to the 1970s and early 1980s, when alcoholic beverage consumption was loosely regulated in the United States. In fact, the minimum drinking age typically ranged from eighteen to twenty-one years depending on the state. Alcohol-related traffic fatalities among young motorists escalated during this time period to the point that concerned citizens felt compelled to mount a social and political campaign to increase public awareness about the problem. By 1984 Mothers Against Drunk Driving (MADD), perhaps the most well known of these groups, had engineered a national debate on the issue. MADD ultimately persuaded Congress and President Ronald Reagan to pass and sign into law the National Minimum Drinking Age Act. The principal objective of this legislation was to induce all fifty states to implement a uniform alcohol purchase age of twenty-one; failure to do so would result in the loss of 10 percent of the state's federal highway funding. Three years later, the U.S. Department of Transportation had determined that all fifty states were in compliance with the act.

In the years since the passage of the Minimum Drinking Age Act, prohibition groups and the federal government have successfully modified prevailing American cultural attitudes toward alcohol consumption. Society as a whole has embraced a number of strategies designed to reduce alcohol-related traffic accidents, including harsh criminal penalties for driving under the influence of alcohol, using a designated driver, and sponsoring public awareness campaigns to educate people about the risks and penalties for drinking and driving. For these groups, the implementation of a uniform minimum legal drinking age in the United States is the cornerstone of a responsible alcohol consumption policy in that it protects teenagers from the dangers of driving under the influence and it delays their exposure to the harmful effects of alcohol. Organizations such as MADD, the Center for Science in the Public Interest, and the National Highway Traffic Safety Administration (NHTSA) have all underscored what they perceive to be the most obvious benefit of the minimum legal drinking age law: It has dramatically reduced alcohol-related traffic fatalities among teenage drivers. Indeed, in 2005 the NHTSA's Center for Statistics and Analysis estimated that minimum drinking age laws have reduced traffic fatalities involving eighteen- to twenty-year-old drivers by 13 percent since 1975. According to the report, this percentage translates into some 24,560 lives saved over a thirty-year span.[3]

In recent years, however, opposition groups have begun to challenge these figures. Leading this effort is John McCardell Jr., the former president of Middlebury College in Vermont and the founder of the nonprofit group Choose Responsibility. This organization's mission is to promote informed public debate and to initiate a fresh analysis of the problem of reckless and excessive drinking among America's youths. Dr. McCardell asserts that the public is being misled about the correlation between the minimum drinking age limit and the overall reduction in teenage traffic fatalities. He points out that a number of factors can be attributed to the reduction in traffic fatalities over the past twenty years, chiefly the increased public awareness about the dangers of drinking and driving that has led to the more frequent use of designated drivers' improvements in Breathalyzer testing and drunken driving law enforcement, and the implementation of automobile safety measures such as mandatory seat belts and air bags. McCardell adds that an analysis of NHTSA data reveals that if anything the enforcement of the minimum legal drinking age limit merely delays the problem: "The most common age for drinking-related deaths is now 21, followed by 22 and 23," he contends. "It seems that the minimum drinking age is as likely to have postponed fatalities as to have reduced them."[4]

Supporters of the minimum legal drinking age law have also argued that it discourages many teenagers from drinking alcohol at a time when their still-developing brains are susceptible to long-term physical damage. In laboratory experiments conducted on adolescent rats, scientists have shown that a pronounced exposure to alcohol leads to such physical problems as impaired decision-making and reasoning skills, inhibited cognitive learning skills, and an inability to make and retain certain memories. Scientific findings vary about how long it takes the human brain to develop—some indicate that the process ends at around the age of twenty, while others maintain that growth continues until age twenty-five. In any case, minimum drinking age advocates contend that encouraging adolescents to delay their first drink of alcohol minimizes the risk of experiencing long-term brain damage.

Minimum-age advocates have also pointed out that scientific research into human behavior supports their position on teenage drinking. Studies show that beginning drinking at an early age increases the likelihood that an adolescent will abuse or become dependent on alcohol and other drugs as an adult. A report issued by the National Institute on Alcohol Abuse and Alcoholism (NIAAA) shows that teenagers who begin drinking before the age of fifteen are four times more likely to become dependent on alcohol later in life than those who wait until they are twenty or older to have their first drinks.[5] Similarly, a national survey published in the *Archives of Pediatrics & Adolescent Medicine* in 2006 indicates that 47 percent of adolescents who begin drinking before the age of fourteen eventually become dependent on alcohol, whereas only 9 percent of people who wait until age twenty-one to have their first drink succumb to alcohol dependence.[6]

Detractors to the legal minimum drinking age dispute the significance of these research findings, with some going so far as to accuse the government of propagating "junk science" to misinform the public. David J. Hanson, professor emeritus of sociology at the State University of New York at Potsdam, is widely regarded as one of the country's leading experts on alcohol and its effects. He maintains that it is scientifically irresponsible to make sweeping conclusions about the negative physical and social consequences of underage drinking based on laboratory animal studies and on studies related to a target group of individuals who are already afflicted by alcohol dependency. Libertarian writer Radley Balko evaluates this scientific dispute in practical terms: "If the research on brain development is true, the U.S. seems to be the only country to have caught on to it. Oddly enough, high school students in much of the rest of the developed world—where lower drinking ages and laxer enforcement reign—do considerably better than U.S. students on standardized tests."[7] McCardell adds that "[there] is a whole slice of the American population today that was allowed to drink at age 18, 19, and 20. Is there any evidence of generational brain impairment among that group? If so, let's see the evidence."[8]

Progressive advocacy groups recommend using common sense when reviewing all of the myths and facts surrounding the minimum drinking age limit. They point out that eighteen-year-olds are old enough to vote, to get married, to sign a legal contract, to join the army, and to smoke cigarettes. Why, they argue, should drinking alcohol be arbitrarily excluded from this list of civil rights? For McCardell and his Choose Responsibility organization, young adults over the age of eighteen should be treated as such. They should be allowed to drink socially with and around older adults who would, in turn, model appropriate alcohol consumption behavior. Further, Choose Responsibility advocates issuing graduated licenses to young adults under the age of twenty-one to ensure that they are receiving the proper education about the health and criminal consequences of alcohol abuse. As McCardell points out, "[Alcohol] education is mandatory now after you've been convicted of driving under the influence. That makes no sense. Why not make it available earlier as a way of preparing young people to deal with alcohol responsibly?"[9]

Proponents for the drinking age rollback admit that they do not know if their approach will result in reduced alcohol abuse and alcohol-related fatalities among teens. However, they are firm in their belief that the present minimum legal drinking age is a failure and that its supporters refuse to engage in a meaningful dialogue about the problem. As Gene Ford, the founder and publisher of *Healthy Drinking* magazine, articulates, "[No] one seriously contends that alcohol should be free of societal controls. The question isn't whether there should be controls, but which controls work best. What has proven around the world to work best is a combination of reasonable laws backed by strong social sanctions. But in the U.S. we treat our emerging adults as infants and get infantile behavior as a result."[10] A 2005 ABC News poll however, indicates that some 78 percent of Americans simply are not ready for such a progressive approach to dealing with teenage alcohol abuse. What is more, even young adults aged thirty-four and under oppose lowering the drinking age below twenty-one.[11] In light of such overwhelming public support for the status quo, it would seem that a substantive reconsideration of the minimum drinking age limit is not likely to happen anytime soon.

Notes

1. Substance Abuse and Mental Health Services Administration, *Results from the 2005 National Survey on Drug Use and Health: National Findings* (NSDUH Series H-30, DHHS Publication No. SMA 06-4194), Rockville, MD: Office of Applied Studies, 2006.
2. Quoted in Karen MacPherson, "National Drinking Age of 21 Successful, Popular." *Pittsburgh Post-Gazette*, July 16, 2005. Article accessed at www.post-gazette.com.
3. "Traffic Safety Facts: 2005 Data," National Highway Traffic Safety Administration (NHTSA), 2005. Report accessed at www-nrd.nhtsa.dot.gov/Pubs/810630.PDF.
4. Quoted in John J. Miller, "The Case Against 21," *National Review*, April 19, 2007. Article accessed at www.nationalreview.com.
5. "Underage Drinking: A Growing Health Concern," National Institute on Alcohol Abuse and Alcoholism (NIAAA), August 2006. Report accessed at pubs.niaaa.nih.gov/publications/PSA/underagepg2.htm.

6. Cited in Kathy Butler, "The Grim Neurology of Teenage Drinking," *New York Times*, July 4, 2006. Article accessed at www.nytimes.com.

7. Radley Balko, "Back to 18?" *Reason Magazine*, April 12, 2007. Article accessed at www.reason.com.

8. Quoted in Sarah Baldauf, "Setting the Bar at 18," *U.S. News & World Report*, April 23, 2007, p. 28.

9. Ibid.

10. Gene Ford, "What About the Drinking Age? Why We Should Lower the Drinking Age to 19," Alcohol: Problems and Solutions, 2002. Article accessed at www2.potsdam.edu/hansondj/YouthIssues/1046348192.html.

11. "Poll: Public Back Legal Drinking Age Limit: After 21 Years of Age-21 Drinking Public Support Remains Strong," ABC News Poll, May 22, 2005. Accessed at http://abcnewsgo.com/Health/PollVault/story?id=941810.

CHAPTER

Effects of Teenage Drinking

The Physical Effects of Alcohol Abuse

Henry Wechsler, PhD and Bernice Wuethrich

In the following viewpoint, Henry Wechsler and Bernice Wuethrich examine the frequency of teenage binge drinking, particularly on college campuses. According to the authors, the harmful physical effects of heavy drinking include hangovers, blackouts, a loss of control, and potentially lethal alcohol poisoning. Moreover, they discuss a number of recent brain development studies that indicate that significant changes occur in the brain during adolescence. Studies also show that alcohol abuse during the teenage years adversely affects areas of the brain that control decision-making and reasoning skills. Alcohol-induced brain damage can also result in slower learning during adolescence and adulthood, the authors report, possibly reducing brain function capability in stressful situations, increasing a desire for pleasure, and locking in or freezing of adolescent patterns of brain functioning. Wechsler and Wuethrich conclude that changing the college drinking environment will significantly impact students' attitudes toward alcohol and counteract the social forces that promote binge drinking.

Consequences of Alcohol Abuse

Few young people seem to worry much about what binge drinking does to themselves or to others. They may routinely shrug off hangovers and even blackouts; laugh off violent, out-of-control behavior; and give in to the pressure—often against their better judgment—for unplanned and unprotected sex. Cirrhosis of the liver, which produces irreversible scarring, seems decades away, and heart disease as remote as

Henry Wechsler, PhD and Bernice Wuethrich, *Dying to Drink: Confronting Binge Drinking on College Campuses*. Emmaus, PA: Rodale, 2002. © 2002 by Henry Wechsler, Ph.D. and Bernice Wuethrich. Reprinted by permission.

retirement. But daily life in campus health centers and nearby emergency rooms shows that bodily harm is not some distant danger. For the binge drinker, it exists in the here and now in the form of alcohol poisoning, assault, and rape.

In addition, new research shows that when it comes to brain function alcohol gives young people plenty to worry about. Teenagers who drink heavily may lose as much as 10 percent of their mental capacity, affecting tasks as varied as learning new information and thinking through complex problems. Because the human brain continues to develop into a person's twenties, excessive drinking even in college has the potential to destroy a significant amount of mental capacity. While research into these effects is new, initial results point to a potentially serious risk in both the short and long term.

Anatomy of a Hangover

Following a night of binge drinking, you will feel the physical aftereffects, even though your body may have already eliminated the alcohol you consumed. (It may not have, too, depending on how much you drank.) You are out of whack. Your internal chemical balance, your digestive organs, the nerves surrounding the lining of your brain, your blood vessels—all are out of balance. You are suffering from a hangover.

A hangover is what happens after prolonged or heavy drinking. It indicates alcohol withdrawal, as the body and brain cells that had adjusted to the presence of alcohol try to adapt to its absence. Just four or five drinks can trigger withdrawal symptoms, which typically kick in between six and forty-eight hours after the last drink. These commonly include headache, nausea, diarrhea, fatigue, muscle pain, jittery hands, and mild anxiety. A more serious form of withdrawal is delirium tremens, or DTs. The DTs typically begin more than forty-eight hours after the last drink and elicit profound confusion, hallucinations, and severe nervous system hyperactivity.

Even a mild hangover can be a ready excuse to skip class or pass up going to the library. It's no wonder then that increased alcohol consumption results in less time spent studying, lower grade point averages, and a greater likelihood of falling behind at school. Our data show that consuming a little more than five drinks per occasion is associated with a half a grade lower GPA [grade point average]. For upperclassmen, adding one more drink increases the probability of getting behind in school by about 5 percent. These results, however, probably under-estimate the problem because they are based on students who were enrolled in colleges at the time of the survey and do not include students who dropped out of college. According to the Core Institute, a nonprofit organization that assists colleges and universities in drug and alcohol prevention efforts, about 159,000 first-year college students will drop out of school for alcohol- or drug-related reasons.

One student told us, "The weekends start on Thursday here, so a big portion of the class is missing on Friday, from hangovers and such things. Drinking and partying take more priority around here than school work does." Another student who drank heavily throughout his first semester as a freshman said, "Fall semester, basically, you just kiss it away."

Blackouts

Thousands of students experience regular warning signals of the damage they are doing to their brains. That warning comes in the form of a blackout.

During an alcohol-induced blackout, the drinker is conscious but forms no memory of events; she may wake up the next morning in a stranger's bed with no clue as to how she got there. This dangerous condition is likely due to alcohol completely shutting down the hippocampus, a deep structure in the brain that is key to learning and memory, said Aaron M. White, Ph.D., a biological psychologist at Duke University Medical Center. Following a blackout, students must rely on the reports of friends or others to know what they did the night before. White surveyed students at one college to learn what kinds of activities they had been involved in during their blackouts. He found that students did everything from spending large amounts of money to engaging in sexual activity to getting in arguments, vandalizing property, and driving a car—all without a memory of what had happened.

Chuck, a junior applying to medical school, described a recent blackout:

> It was a week after my twenty-first birthday, and we had been snowed in all week. I hadn't had a chance to go to a bar yet. When we finally went out to celebrate, I had four drinks in my dorm room before we left. At the bar there was some kind of sorority event. I had fifteen or sixteen drinks in a three-hour period. The last thing I remember— the drinks were really strong—I finished my drink and asked for another. I apparently continued to dance. I danced in a cage and spun on the floor. I was dancing with all these girls. A friend jumped on my back in the parking lot and we went running around piggyback. Apparently my friends tried to drive me home. But I had to get out of the car. Apparently I got sick and I was face-down in the snow throwing up. I was so sick that I wouldn't get back in the car. My best friend half-carried, half-walked me home. I went to visit a friend in my dorm; I climbed into bed with him. I don't remember any of this. There are pictures of me hovering over the toilet. I woke up the next morning with a garbage pail full of vomit next to my bed. I don't remember any of this. I was hungover for a day and a half. It's funny—we laugh about it. But really I could have been very close to being dead there. It's not a funny situation.

In the past researchers assumed that blackouts were an indicator of alcoholism. Now, however, they are realizing just how common blackouts are among nonalcoholics. In our College Alcohol Study, one out of every four students who drank reported having forgotten where they were or what they did while drinking during the school year. The incidence of blackout more than doubled, to 54 percent, among frequent binge drinkers. The White study also found that female students experience blackouts at far lower doses of alcohol than males. The average alcohol intake of females who blacked out was five drinks per occasion, while that of males was nine drinks per occasion.

A Loss of Control

Chuck's friends told him about what happened during another one of his blackouts:

> I was sitting on the porch; I threw a beer on my friend and he threw a beer on me. The last thing I remember was a beer hitting me in my face. The next think I knew I was in the shower. They told me that they had locked me on the porch and thrown a barrel of beer on me. I was trying to get in, they opened the door, and they doused me in a bucket of ice-cold water. I sat back down, said something to the effect that I don't want all this beer to go to waste. I was dumping it on me. 1 put the keg hose in my pants. I don't remember that five- to ten-minute period. It's like it never happened.

Some students realize that blackouts are a danger sign, if for no other reason than that they signal a total loss of control. As Leslie, a junior at a Jesuit college said, "I don't know why you'd get to the point where you can't remember what happened the night before. If you have to ask, Did I hook up with so and so, How did I get home, Who drove with whom? . . . Are you kidding me? I ask my friends, Why would you get to that point?"

Whether one's experiences and behavior during blackouts are "harmless" or extreme, a blackout is a warning that fundamental changes are taking place in the brain. Some of those changes are transient, others may last a lifetime, yet few students have an accurate understanding of either set of effects.

Alcohol and the Teenage Brain

Scientists know that long-term excessive alcohol consumption by adults can cause brain damage ranging from a mild loss of motor skills to psychosis and even the inability to form memories. Until recently we have had no clue as to the effects of alcohol on the brain during adolescence—that period of transition from childhood to adulthood that spans the second decade of life.

Because the brain reaches 95 percent of its final size by age five, scientists had for a long time assumed that most development was also complete by that age. Now we know that while the total size changes little after age five, the parts that make up the brain go through some major remodeling during the teenage years.

The Cement Is Still Setting

It has been hard to study the teenage brain. Teen mortality is low, and autopsies are rarely performed. A major source of information on brain development is the Yakovlev-Haleem Brain Collection housed at the Walter Reed Army Medical Center in Washington, D.C. Begun in 1930, the collection includes hundreds of adult brains but just eleven brains of children who died between the ages of three and eighteen. "A lot of what has been known about teen brains has been based on these eleven brains," said Jay Giedd at the National Institute of Mental Health in Bethesda, Maryland.

Beginning in the 1990s, Giedd used a noninvasive technique called magnetic resonance imaging to study the living brains of more than eight hundred people between the ages of three and eighteen. Every two years he scanned their developing brains, and he now has more than twenty-five hundred images showing developmental patterns.

"Adolescence is a very busy, tumultuous time in the brain; its wiring is laid down much later than we used to think," Giedd said. "Since the cement of the brain is still setting, if teenagers do use alcohol or drugs they may not just be affecting their brain for that night or weekend, but for the next eighty years of their life."

Tumultuous Times

Two of the most noticeable changes occur in the brain's prefrontal cortex and in its limbic system. The prefrontal cortex, located behind the forehead, is the brain's chief decision-maker and voice of reason. The limbic system includes the brain's hippocampus, a wishbone-shaped structure that is responsible for many types of learning and memory, and the amygdala, which responds to matters of life and death. It is mobilized when a person is hungry or frightened or angry and helps the brain process such survival impulses. Both the prefrontal cortex and the limbic system must be able to work in concert for a person to make sound decisions.

During adolescence, the prefrontal cortex changes more than any other part of the brain. At around age eleven or twelve its nerve cells, or neurons, branch out like crazy, only to be seriously pruned back in the years that follow. All this tumult is to good purpose. In the adult brain the prefrontal cortex executes the thought processes younger people struggle to master: the ability to plan ahead, think abstractly, and integrate information to make sound decisions. It transforms from functioning in a more global to a more specialized way.

In teenagers the hippocampus is loaded with estrogen receptors and grows larger in girls than in boys during these years. On the other hand, the amygdala is loaded with testosterone receptors and grows more rapidly in boys. These changes continue up until age twenty in some young people, Giedd said.

Now, researchers are seeing some of the worst alcohol-related brain damage occurring in these parts of the brain during the teenage years. One disturbing finding is that alcohol-induced cell death and damage shrinks the hippocampus. Michael De Bellis at the University of Pittsburgh Medical Center used magnetic resonance imaging to compare the hippocampi of youth from fourteen to twenty-one years of age who abused alcohol to those who did not. The longer and the more a young person had been drinking, the smaller his hippocampus. The average size difference between healthy teenagers and alcohol abusers was roughly 10 percent. That's a lot of lost brain cells.

Short- and Long-Term Effects

Pharmacologist Fulton Crews, director of the Center for Alcohol Studies at the University of North Carolina in Chapel Hill, has investigated the different patterns of brain cell death in adolescents and adults by studying rats. While juvenile and adult rats both showed severe damage in the back areas of the brain and the frontally located olfactory bulb after four-day drinking bouts, only the adolescents suffered brain damage in other frontal areas, and that damage was severe. The regions of cell death in the rat experiment correspond to the human prefrontal cortex and to parts of the limbic system, which is especially worrisome because they play an important role in the formation of an adult personality. "Binge drinking could be making permanent long-term changes in the final neural physiology, which is expressed as personality and behavior in the individual," Crews said.

Another set of experiments by neuropsychologist Scott Swartzwelder at Duke University has shown that alcohol disrupts a brain process called long-term potentiation, or LTP, more severely in adolescent than in adult rats. Scientists think that an LTP-type process is necessary for the brain to form memories. Swartzwelder found that exposure to the equivalent of just two beers inhibits this process in adolescent rats while it takes more than twice as much beer to similarly inhibit adult rats. These findings led him to suspect that alcohol consumption might retard learning in adolescents.

To see whether this was true for humans, Swartzwelder recruited a group of volunteers aged twenty-one to twenty-nine years old. (He could not use younger volunteers because drinking is illegal for those under age twenty-one.) He split the volunteers into two groups: twenty-one to twenty-four years old, and twenty-five to twenty-nine years old. After just three drinks, with a blood-alcohol level slightly below .08 percent, the younger group's learning was impaired 25 percent more than the older group's. "The adolescent brain is a developing nervous system," summarized Swartzwelder, "and the things you do to it can change it."

To find out if heavy alcohol consumption could cause long-term cognitive damage in bingeing adolescents, Swartzwelder's colleague, Aaron White, devised another experiment. He gave adolescent and adult rats very large doses of alcohol every other day for twenty days—the rough equivalent of a 150-pound human chugging twenty-four drinks in a row. Twenty days after the last binge, when the adolescent rats had reached adulthood, White trained them in a maze memory task. Both the younger and older rats performed equally well when sober. But when intoxicated, those who had binged as adolescents performed much worse. "Binge exposure to alcohol during adolescence appears to produce long-lasting changes in brain function," White said. He suspects that the early damage caused by alcohol could surface *whenever* the brain is taxed or stressed, not just when it is again challenged by alcohol.

The collective damage caused by having so many American adolescents reach for one drink after another may be incalculable. "People in their late teens have been drinking heavily for generations. We're not a society of idiots, but we're not a society of Einsteins either," said Swartzwelder. "What if you've compromised your function by 7 percent or 10 percent and never known the difference?"

Memory Problems

Taking another approach, Sandra Brown, Susan Tapert, and Gregory Brown at the University of California, San Diego, and the VA [Veterans Administration] San Diego Health Care System have been following a group of thirty-three teenagers—all heavy drinkers—for eight years. Repeated testing shows that these problem drinkers perform more poorly on tests of cognition and learning than do nondrinkers.

On average, each teen had used alcohol more than seven hundred fifty times—the equivalent of drinking every day for two and a half years. Bingeing was common: The teens downed an average of eight drinks at each sitting. The researchers matched drinkers with nondrinkers of the same gender and similar age, IQ, socioeconomic background, and family history of alcohol. Then, three weeks after the drinkers had their last drink, all the teens took a two-hour battery of tests.

The teens with alcohol problems had a harder time recalling information, both verbal and nonverbal, that they had learned just twenty minutes earlier. Words such as *apple* and *football* escaped them. The performance difference was about 10 percent. "It's not serious brain damage, but it's the difference of a grade, a pass or a fail," Tapert said. Other tests evaluated skills needed for map learning, geometry, and science. Again, there was a 10 percent difference in performance.

Furthermore, Tapert and Sandra Brown found the single best predictor of neuropsychological deficits for the adolescents was withdrawal symptoms, and that just several years of heavy alcohol altered their brain functions in ways that hamper learning. In other words, those young people that experience regular hangovers—a result of the brain's withdrawal from alcohol—are at higher risk of learning deficits. This is especially true of those youth who experience the most extreme withdrawal, DTs.

Sandra Brown is following the teens until they reach age thirty, and some have already passed twenty-one. "Those who continue to use alcohol heavily are developing attentional deficits in addition to the memory and problem-solving deficits that showed up early on," she said. "In the past we thought of alcohol as a more benign drug. It's not included in the war on drugs. This clearly demonstrates that the most popular drug is also an incredibly dangerous drug."

Premature Pleasure

Sandra Brown's research team is also using a brain imaging technique called functional magnetic resonance imaging to compare the brain function of alcohol abusers and nondrinkers. Initial results show that the brains of young adults with a history of alcohol dependence are less active than those of nondrinkers during tasks that require spatial working memory, such as being able to remember the location of your car in a large parking garage. In addition, the adolescent drinkers seem to exhibit greater levels of brain activity when they are exposed to alcohol-related stimuli. For instance, when the drinkers read words such as *wasted* or *tequila* on a screen, the nucleus accumbens—a small section of the brain associated with craving—lights up.

The nucleus accumbens is integral to the brain's so-called pleasure circuit, which scientists now believe also undergoes major remodeling during adolescence. Underlying the pleasure circuit is the neurotransmitter dopamine, a natural chemical in the brain. Sex, food, and many drugs, including alcohol, can all induce the release of dopamine, which creates feelings of pleasure and in turn encourages repetition of the original behavior.

During adolescence, the balance of dopamine activity temporarily shifts away from the nucleus accumbens, the brain's key pleasure and reward center, to the prefrontal cortex. Linda Spear, a developmental psychobiologist at Binghamton University in New York, speculates that as a result of this shift in balance, adolescents may find drugs less rewarding than they would earlier or later in life. And if the drugs produce less of a kick, more would be needed to get the same effect. "In the case of alcohol, this may lead to binge drinking," she said.

Can the Brain Bounce Back?

In adult alcoholics, some alcohol-related brain damage will reverse with abstinence and time. For example, at least some lost brain volume will be restored. Also, one study found that cognitively impaired alcoholic patients use different brain pathways than unimpaired patients to complete the same mental tasks. In essence, the brain rerouted its mental traffic from damaged routes to routes that had previously been reserved for other tasks. This resilience offers hope, but no one knows whether damage done by alcohol to the adolescent brain can be overcome in the same way. Damage from alcohol could arrest the teenage brain's development and lock in adolescent patterns of brain functioning.

To test this possibility, Swartzwelder and White recently conducted another test with rats. Adolescents—rats *and* human—suffer less immediate motor impairment during a drinking session than do adults. In other words, adolescents must drink more than adults to lose their balance and fall over. As both people and rats age, however, they become more susceptible to alcohol-induced motor impairment. The experiment found that repeated bingeing by young rats locked in the adolescent pattern of motor-control response to alcohol. Even after reaching adulthood, the rats that binged in their youth remained less affected by alcohol in their motor responses. This suggests that other neural circuitry may also become frozen in time as a result of heavy alcohol use while young.

Young and Addicted

As we have seen, alcohol changes the brain in many ways. It can even cause changes that discourage one from stopping drinking. For example, repeated alcohol use makes it harder for an individual to learn new ways of doing things, rather than repeating the same actions over and over again. In short, it becomes increasingly difficult to stop reaching for beer after beer after beer.

Alcohol works these changes through altering our brain chemistry. Alcoholism, or alcohol dependence, is not a result of moral weakness; it is a physiological addiction and a disease that if left unchecked will get progressively worse. Individuals may be genetically predisposed to alcoholism, but if anyone puts enough alcohol into his or her brain over a long enough time, he or she will become physically dependent on the drug.

The essence of addiction is an inability to stop taking a drug regardless of its consequences. A student could be flunking out of school, ruining friendships, spending money needed for books and food on alcohol instead, and still continue drinking. The alcoholic knows he is hurting himself and others but cannot stop, even when he tries. The condition generally includes four symptoms:

- *Craving*: a strong need, or compulsion, to drink.

- *Impaired control*: the inability to limit one's drinking on any given occasion.

- *Physical dependence*: withdrawal symptoms, such as nausea, sweating, shakiness, and anxiety, when alcohol use is stopped after a period of heavy drinking.

- *Tolerance*: the need for increasing amounts of alcohol in order to feel its effects. About 6 percent of the students in our survey—and one in every five frequent binge drinkers—can be diagnosed as alcohol dependent. Alcohol dependence is a chronic and often progressive disease that runs a generally predictable course with recognizable symptoms. About 31 percent of students can be diagnosed as alcohol abusers. Alcohol abuse is a harmful drinking pattern that continues despite having persistent social or interpersonal problems caused or exacerbated by the effects of alcohol use. Students who were frequent binge drinkers were eighteen times more likely to be impaired than drinkers who didn't binge.

Some students know they have a problem but don't know where to go for help or what to do. Many more students are aware of friends with alcohol problems. One Cornell student described alcohol this way: "It's insidious and it sneaks up on people. My understanding is colored by the fact that my father drinks too much, and he started doing so in college." A student from Dartmouth reflected, "It's very sad to think that you became an alcoholic because you went to college."

We know that the younger a person is when he starts to drink, the more likely he is to experience a range of problems, including alcohol dependence, later in life. A study by the National Epidemiologic Survey found that approximately 40 percent of the drinkers who got started before age fifteen were classified later in life as alcohol dependent, compared to only 10 percent of those who began drinking at age twenty-one or twenty-two. Overall, beginning at age fifteen, the risk of future alcohol dependence decreased by 14 percent with each passing year of abstention.

When college administrations, parents, or students accept underage drinking as a fact of life, they are paving the road to futures of ongoing alcohol problems and possibly compromised intellectual ability. When the alcohol industry argues that alcohol is not a drug and fights for its right to advertise on campus and promote cheap drink specials, it is ensuring a steady supply of future customers—the most loyal of whom will be addicts.

While recovery from alcoholism is possible—and treatment must be made available to young people who have already developed alcohol problems—only changing the college drinking environment will prevent large numbers of students from sacrificing their potential to the beer or liquor bottle.

What Teens Should Know Before Taking a Drink

Nemours Foundation

Philanthropist Alfred I. Du Pont founded the Nemours Foundation in 1936, an organization committed to improving the health of children. The Nemours Foundation established the KidsHealth Web site in 1995 as an online resource to provide accurate and up-to-date health information for families with children and teenagers. The following KidsHealth article discusses how alcohol is made and how it affects the human brain via the central nervous system. It presents reasons why teens should not drink and proposes methods for kids to avoid drinking in peer pressure situations. The article also discusses methods that teens can use to help others with drinking problems.

Just about everyone knows that the legal drinking age throughout the United States is 21. But according to the National Center on Addiction and Substance Abuse, almost 80% of high school students have tried alcohol.

Deciding whether to drink is a personal decision that we each eventually have to make. This article provides some information on alcohol, including how it affects your body, so you can make an educated choice.

What Is Alcohol?

Alcohol is created when grains, fruits, or vegetables are fermented. Fermentation is a process that uses yeast or bacteria to change the sugars in the food into alcohol. Fermentation is

Nemours Foundation, "TeensHealth: Alcohol," www.kidshealth.org, November 2006. Copyright © 1995–2007, The Nemours Foundation/KidsHealth. Reprinted with the permission from www.teenshealth.org.

used to produce many necessary items—everything from cheese to medications. Alcohol has different forms and can be used as a cleaner, an antiseptic, or a sedative.

So if alcohol is a natural product, why do teens need to be concerned about drinking it? When people drink alcohol, it's absorbed into their bloodstream. From there, it affects the central nervous system (the brain and spinal cord), which controls virtually all body functions. Because experts now know that the human brain is still developing during our teens, scientists are researching the effects drinking alcohol can have on the teen brain.

How Does It Affect the Body?

Alcohol is a depressant, which means it slows the function of the central nervous system. Alcohol actually blocks some of the messages trying to get to the brain. This alters a person's perceptions, emotions, movement, vision, and healing.

In very small amounts, alcohol can help a person feel more relaxed or less anxious. More alcohol causes greater changes in the brain, resulting in intoxication. People who have overused alcohol may stagger, lose their coordination, and slur their speech. They will probably be confused and disoriented. Depending on the person, intoxication can make someone very friendly and talkative or very aggressive and angry. Reaction times are slowed dramatically—which is why people are told not to drink and drive. People who are intoxicated may think they're moving properly when they're not. They may act totally out of character.

When large amounts of alcohol are consumed in a short period of time, alcohol poisoning can result. Alcohol poisoning is exactly what it sounds like—the body has become poisoned by large amounts of alcohol. Violent vomiting is usually the first symptom of alcohol poisoning. Extreme sleepiness, unconsciousness, difficulty breathing, dangerously low blood sugar, seizures, and even death may result.

Why Do Teens Drink?

Experimentation with alcohol during the teen years is common. Some reasons that teens use alcohol and other drugs are:

- curiosity

- to feel good, reduce stress, and relax

- to fit in

- to feel older

From a very young age, kids see advertising messages showing beautiful people enjoying life—and alcohol. And because many parents and other adults use alcohol socially—having beer or wine with dinner, for example—alcohol seems harmless to many teens.

Why Shouldn't I Drink?

Although it's illegal to drink alcohol in the United States until the age of 21, most teens can get access to it. It's therefore up to you to make a decision about drinking. In addition to the possibility of becoming addicted, there are some downsides to drinking:

The punishment is severe. Teens who drink put themselves at risk for obvious problems with the law (it's illegal; you can get arrested). Teens who drink are also more likely to get into fights and commit crimes than those who don't.

People who drink regularly also often have problems with school. Drinking can damage a student's ability to study well and get decent grades, as well as affect sports performance (the coordination thing).

You can look really stupid. The impression is that drinking is cool, but the nervous system changes that come from drinking alcohol can make people do stupid or embarrassing things, like throwing up or peeing on themselves. Drinking also gives people bad breath, and no one enjoys a hangover.

Alcohol puts you at risk. Teens who drink are more likely to be sexually active and to have unsafe, unprotected sex. Resulting pregnancies and sexually transmitted diseases can change—or even end—lives. The risk of injuring yourself, maybe even fatally, is higher when you're under the influence, too. One half of all drowning deaths among teen guys are related to alcohol use. Use of alcohol greatly increases the chance that a teen will be involved in a car crash, homicide, or suicide.

Teen drinkers are more likely to get fat or have health problems, too. One study by the University of Washington found that people who regularly had five or more drinks in a row starting at age 13 were much more likely to be overweight or have high blood pressure by age 24 than their nondrinking peers. People who continue drinking heavily well into adulthood risk damaging their organs, such as the liver, heart, and brain.

How Can I Avoid Drinking?

If all your friends drink and you don't want to, it can be hard to say "no, thanks." No one wants to risk feeling rejected or left out. Different strategies for turning down alcohol work for different people. Some people find it helps to say no without giving an explanation, others think offering their reasons works better ("I'm not into drinking," "I have a game tomorrow," or "my uncle died from drinking," for example).

If saying no to alcohol makes you feel uncomfortable in front of people you know, blame your parents or another adult for your refusal. Saying, "My parents are coming to pick me up soon," "I already got in major trouble for drinking once, I can't do it again," or "my coach would kill me," can make saying no a bit easier for some.

If you're going to a party and you know there will be alcohol, plan your strategy in advance. You and a friend can develop a signal for when it's time to leave, for example. You can also make sure that you have plans to do something besides just hanging out in someone's basement drinking beer all night. Plan a trip to the movies, the mall, a concert or a sports event. You might also organize your friends into a volleyball, bowling, or softball team—any activity that gets you moving.

Girls or guys who have strong self-esteem are less likely to become problem drinkers than people with low self-esteem.

Where Can I Get Help?

If you think you have a drinking problem, get help as soon as possible. The best approach is to talk to an adult you trust. If you can't approach your parents, talk to your doctor, school counselor, clergy member, aunt, or uncle. It can be hard for some people to talk to adults about these issues, but a supportive person in a position to help can refer students to a drug and alcohol counselor for evaluation and treatment.

In some states, this treatment is completely confidential. After assessing a teen's problem, a counselor may recommend a brief stay in rehab or outpatient treatment. These treatment centers help a person gradually overcome the physical and psychological dependence on alcohol.

What If I'm Concerned About Someone Else's Drinking?

Many people live in homes where a parent or other family member drinks too much. This may make you angry, scared, and depressed. Many people can't control their drinking without help. This doesn't mean that they love or care about you any less. Alcoholism is an illness that needs to be treated just like other illnesses.

People with drinking problems can't stop drinking until they are ready to admit they have a problem and get help. This can leave family members and loved ones feeling helpless. The good news is there are many places to turn for help: a supportive adult, such as your guidance counselor, or a relative or older sibling will understand what you're going through. Also, professional organizations like Alateen can help.

If you have a friend whose drinking concerns you, make sure he or she stays safe. Don't let your friend drink and drive, for example. If you can, try to keep friends who have been drinking from doing anything dangerous, such as trying to walk home at night alone or starting a fight. And protect yourself, too. Don't get in a car with someone who's been drinking, even if that person is your ride home. Ask a sober adult to drive you instead or call a cab.

Everyone makes decisions about whether to drink and how much—even adults. It's possible to enjoy a party or other event just as much, if not more so, when you don't drink. And with your central nervous system working as it's supposed to, you'll remember more about the great time you had!

How Alcohol Can Damage a Developing Brain

Kathy Butler

Kathy Butler reports on a number of recent scientific studies and laboratory experiments that have examined how teenage alcohol abuse impacts long-term brain development. According to these studies, teenage alcoholics suffer verbal and nonverbal memory loss, increased attention deficit, and a decreased ability to exercise spatial skills. Further, the findings demonstrate how alcohol consumption affects adolescent and adult brains differently, noting that while developing brains demonstrate the capacity to shift key cognitive functions away from cells damaged by alcohol, nevertheless the damage caused by alcohol impairs the development of critical thinking and inhibits the generation of new brain cells. It is too soon to draw firm conclusions about the long-term effects of alcohol abuse, Butler observes, but research suggests that quitting drinking altogether is the best way to prevent further damage to the brain.

Teenagers have been drinking alcohol for centuries. In pre-Revolutionary America, young apprentices were handed buckets of ale. In the 1890's, at the age of 15, the writer Jack London regularly drank grown sailors under the table.

For almost as long, concerned adults have tried to limit teenage alcohol consumption. In the 1830's, temperance societies administered lifelong abstinence pledges to schoolchildren. Today, public health experts regularly warn that teenage drinkers run greatly increased risks of involvement in car accidents, fights and messy scenes in Cancún [Mexico].

But what was once a social and moral debate may soon become a neurobiological one.

The Neurobiological Effects of Teenage Drinking

The costs of early heavy drinking, experts say, appear to extend far beyond the time that drinking takes away from doing homework, dating, acquiring social skills, and the related tasks of growing up.

Mounting research suggests that alcohol causes more damage to the developing brains of teenagers than was previously thought, injuring them significantly more than it does adult brains. The findings, though preliminary, have demolished the assumption that people can drink heavily for years before causing themselves significant neurological injury. And the research even suggests that early heavy drinking may undermine the precise neurological capacities needed to protect oneself from alcoholism.

The new findings may help explain why people who begin drinking at an early age face enormous risks of becoming alcoholics. According to the results of a national survey of 43,093 adults, published . . . [July 3, 2006] in *Archives of Pediatrics & Adolescent Medicine,* 47 percent of those who begin drinking alcohol before the age of 14 become alcohol dependent at some time in their lives, compared with 9 percent of those who wait at least until age 21. The correlation holds even when genetic risks for alcoholism are taken into account.

The most alarming evidence of physical damage comes from federally financed laboratory experiments on the brains of adolescent rats subjected to binge doses of alcohol. These studies found significant cellular damage to the forebrain and the hippocampus.

And although it is unclear how directly these findings can be applied to humans, there is some evidence to suggest that young alcoholics may suffer analogous deficits.

Alcoholism and Memory Loss

Studies conducted over the last eight years by federally financed researchers in San Diego, for example, found that alcoholic teenagers performed poorly on tests of verbal and nonverbal memory, attention focusing and exercising spatial skills like those required to read a map or assemble a precut bookcase.

"There is no doubt about it now: there are long-term cognitive consequences to excessive drinking of alcohol in adolescence," said Aaron White, an assistant research professor in the psychiatry department at Duke University and the co-author of a recent study of extreme drinking on college campuses.

"We definitely didn't know 5 or 10 years ago that alcohol affected the teen brain differently," said Dr. White, who has also been involved in research at Duke on alcohol in adolescent rats. "Now there's a sense of urgency. It's the same place we were in when everyone realized what a bad thing it was for pregnant women to drink alcohol."

One of two brain areas known to be affected is the hippocampus, a structure crucial for learning and memory. In 1995, Dr. White and other researchers placed delicate sensors inside living brain slices from the hippocampi of adolescent rats and discovered that alcohol drastically suppressed the activity of specific chemical receptors in the region.

Normally, these receptors are activated by the neurotransmitter glutamate and allow calcium to enter neurons, setting off a cascade of changes that strengthen synapses, by helping to create repeated connections between cells, aiding in the efficient formation of new memories.

Alcohol Affects Adolescent and Adult Brain Cells Differently

But at the equivalent of one or two alcoholic drinks, the receptors' activity slowed, and at higher doses, they shut down almost entirely. The researchers, led by Scott Swartzwelder, a neuropsychologist at Duke and at the Veterans Affairs Medical Center in Durham, N.C., found that the suppressive effect was significantly stronger in adolescent rat brain cells than in the brain cells of adult rats.

As might be predicted, the cellular shutdown affected the ability of the younger rats to learn and remember. In other experiments, the team found that adolescent rats under the influence of alcohol had far more trouble than did tipsy adult rats when required repeatedly to locate a platform submerged in a tub of cloudy water and swim to it.

The High Frequency of Blackouts Among Teenage Drinkers

Dr. Swartzwelder said it was likely that in human teenagers, analogous neural mechanisms might explain alcohol "blackouts"—a lack of memory for events that occur during a night of heavy drinking without a loss of consciousness. Blackouts were once thought to be a symptom of advanced adult alcoholism, but researchers have recently discovered just how frequent they are among teenagers as well.

In a 2002 e-mail survey of 772 Duke undergraduates, Dr. White and Dr. Swartzwelder found that 51 percent of those who drank at all had had at least one blackout in their drinking lifetimes; they reported an average of three blackouts apiece.

These averages barely suggest the frequency of blackouts among young adults at the extreme end of the drinking scale. Toren Volkmann, 26, is a graduate of the University of San Diego who, at 14, started drinking heavily almost every weekend and at 24 checked himself into a residential alcohol treatment program.

"It was common for me to basically black out at least once or twice every weekend in late high school and definitely through college, and it wasn't a big deal to me," said Mr. Volkmann, a co-author, with his mother, Chris, of *From Binge to Blackout: A Mother and Son Struggle with Teen Drinking*, . . . published in August [2006] "I wouldn't even worry about what happened, because I wouldn't know."

Blackouts are usually mercifully brief, and once they are over, the capacity to form new memories returns. But younger rats subjected to binge drinking also displayed subtler long-term problems in learning and memory, the researchers found, even after they were allowed to grow up and "dry out."

Lab Tests Indicate Long-Term Problems Associated with Drinking

In experiments conducted by the Duke team, the reformed rat drinkers learned mazes normally when they were sober. But after the equivalent of only a couple of drinks, their performance declined significantly more than did that of rats that had never tippled before they became adults. The study was published in 2000 in the journal *Alcoholism: Clinical and Experimental Research*. Other research has found that while drunken adolescent rats become more sensitive to memory impairment, their hippocampal cells become less responsive than adults' to the neurotransmitter gamma-amino butyric acid, or GABA, which helps induce calmness and sleepiness.

This cellular mechanism may help explain Jack London's observation, in *John Barleycorn: Alcoholic Memoirs* that when he was a teenager he could keep drinking long after his adult companions fell asleep.

"Clearly, something is changed in the brain by early alcohol exposure," Dr. Swartzwelder said in an interview. "It's a double-edged sword and both of the edges are bad.

"Teenagers can drink far more than adults before they get sleepy enough to stop, but along the way they're impairing their cognitive functions much more powerfully."

Teenage Drinking Alters Critical Thinking Development

Alcohol also appears to damage more severely the frontal areas of the adolescent brain, crucial for controlling impulses and thinking through consequences of intended actions— capacities many addicts and alcoholics of all ages lack.

In 2000, Fulton Crews, a neuropharmacologist at the University of North Carolina, subjected adolescent and adult rats to the equivalent of a four-day alcoholic binge and then autopsied them, sectioning their forebrains and staining them with a silver solution to identify dead neurons.

All the rats showed some cell die-off in the forebrain, but the damage was at least twice as severe in the forebrains of the adolescent rats, and it occurred in some areas that were entirely spared in the adults.

Although human brains are far more developed and elaborate in their frontal regions, some functions are analogous across species, Dr. Crews said, including planning and impulse control. During human adolescence, these portions of the brain are heavily remolded and rewired, as teenagers learn—often excruciatingly slowing—how to exercise adult decision-making skills, like the ability to focus, to discriminate, to predict and to ponder questions of right and wrong.

"Alcohol creates disruption in parts of the brain essential for self-control, motivation and goal setting," Dr. Crews said, and can compound pre-existing genetic and psychological vulnerabilities. "Early drinking is affecting a sensitive brain in a way that promotes the progression to addiction.

"Let's say you've been arrested for driving while drunk and spent seven days in jail," Dr. Crews said. "You'd think, 'No way am I going to speed and drive drunk again,' because you have the ability to weigh the consequences and the importance of a behavior. This is exactly what addicts don't do."

Alcohol Prevents the Creation of Nerve Cells

In another experiment, published this year [2006] in the journal *Neuroscience*, Dr. Crews found that even a single high dose of alcohol temporarily prevented the creation of new nerve cells from progenitor stem cells in the forebrain that appear to be involved in brain development.

The damage, far more serious in adolescent rats than in adult rats, began at a level equivalent to two drinks in humans and increased steadily as the dosage was increased to the equivalent of 10 beers, when it stopped the production of almost all new nerve cells.

Dr. Crews added, however, that adult alcoholics who stop drinking are known to recover cognitive function over time.

The same may hold true for hard-drinking teenagers. In 1998, Sandra Brown and Susan Tapert, clinical psychologists at the University of California, San Diego, and at the Veterans Affairs Medical Center there, found that 15-to-16-year-olds who said they had been drunk at least 100 times performed significantly more poorly than their matched nondrinking peers on tests of verbal and nonverbal memory.

The teenagers, who were sober during the testing, had been drunk an average of 750 times in the course of their young lives.

"Heavy alcohol involvement during adolescence is associated with cognitive deficits that worsen as drinking continues into late adolescence and young adulthood," Dr. Tapert said.

Two M.R.I. scan studies [magnetic resonance imaging used to study internal organs], one conducted by Dr. Tapert, have found that hard-drinking teenagers had significantly smaller hippocampi than their sober counterparts. But it is also possible, the researchers said, that the heavy drinkers had smaller hippocampi even before they started to drink.

Damaged Brains Try to Adapt

Teenagers who drink heavily may also use their brains differently to make up for subtle neurological damage, Dr. Tapert said. A study using functional M.R.I. scans, published in 2004, found that alcohol-abusing teenagers who were given a spatial test showed more activation in the parietal regions of the brain, toward the back of the skull, than did nondrinking teenagers.

When female drinkers in the group were tested in their early 20's, their performance declined significantly in comparison with nondrinkers, and their brains showed less activation than normal in the frontal and parietal regions.

Dr. Tapert hypothesized that when the drinkers were younger, their brains had been able to recruit wider areas of the brain for the task.

"This is a fairly sensitive measure of early stages of subtle neuronal disruption, and it is likely to be rectifiable if the person stops drinking," Dr. Tapert said.

The good news is that the brain is remarkably plastic, she added, and future studies may show that the teenage brain, while more vulnerable to the effects of alcohol, is also more resilient.

She pointed to test results from the original group of teenagers, recruited from substance abuse treatment centers and brought into the lab when they were 15 by Dr. Brown. When Dr. Tapert retested the teenagers eight years later, those who had relapsed and who continued to get drunk frequently performed the worst on tests requiring focused attention, while those who reported the most hangovers performed the worst on spatial tasks.

On the other hand, the relative handful of teenagers and young adults in the group who stayed sober—28 percent of the total—performed almost as well, at both the four-year and the eight-year mark, as other San Diego teenagers who had rarely, if ever, had a drink.

Quitting Drinking Can Restore Many Cognitive Functions

Mr. Volkmann, the University of San Diego graduate, was not part of Dr. Tapert's study. While in college, Mr. Volkmann said, he thought he drank for the fun of it. His moment of truth came in the Peace Corps in Paraguay, when he began waking up with sweats and tremors. He discovered he could not control his drinking even when he wanted.

The son of an anesthesiologist and a former teacher in Olympia, Wash., Mr. Volkmann spent a month in a residential treatment program and six months in a halfway house. He has since returned to San Diego.

He said in an interview that he had no way of knowing exactly how drinking affected his overall brain function. But on one point, he is clear.

"My memory is definitely better now," he said. "Every day now, I can count on the fact that when I think back to the night before, I know what happened."

Adolescents and Alcohol Are a Dangerous Mix

National Institute on Alcohol Abuse and Alcoholism (NIAAA)

The National Institute on Alcohol Abuse and Alcoholism (NIAAA) is a federal government agency that conducts research, collaborates with other research institutes, and disseminates findings on alcohol-related problems. The following article produced by the NIAAA discusses the scope of the underage-drinking problem in the United States today, and observes that serious problems are more likely to develop later in life when drinking begins at an early age. The article outlines the principal dangers of adolescent alcohol use, including drinking and driving, suicide, sexual assault, and high-risk sexual activity. To combat the onset of drinking at a young age, the NIAAA supports programs that focus on early intervention.

Underage alcohol use isn't limited to frat houses and football games. In fact the age at which kids start experimenting with alcohol is younger than ever. By the time they reach the eighth grade, nearly half of all adolescents have had at least one drink, and over 20 percent report having been "drunk." A recent study of 12th graders showed that nearly a third of these students "binge" drink' that is, they reported drinking at least five drinks at one time within the last 2 weeks.

Apart from being illegal, underage drinking is risky business—to both the drinker and the community. Each drink increases the total crash risk more among drivers under 21 than drivers 21 and older. Adolescents who drink also may be at greater risk for alcohol-induced brain damage, which could lead to poor performance at school or work. Moreover, a per-

National Institute on Alcohol Abuse and Alcoholism (NIAAA), "Underage Drinking: A Growing Health Concern," August 2006.

son who starts drinking at an early age is more likely to develop serious alcohol problems, including alcoholism, later in life.

Preventing underage drinking continues to be central to the mission of the National Institute on Alcohol Abuse and Alcoholism (NIAAA). NIAAA supports research aimed at developing early intervention approaches that will prevent alcohol problems among youth, especially those between the ages of 12 and 20. Helping people understand the significance of this problem is an important component of this initiative. This publication describes the scope of underage drinking today, including the most harmful consequences, as well as prevention and treatment approaches that are proving particularly effective in meeting the needs of this age group.

The Dangers of Adolescent Alcohol Use

Underage alcohol use is more likely to kill young people than all illegal drugs combined. Some of the most serious and widespread alcohol-related problems among adolescents are described below.

Drinking and Driving. Motor vehicle crashes are the leading cause of death among youth ages 15 to 20. Adolescents already are at increased risk through their relative lack of driving experience, and drivers younger than 21 are more susceptible than older drivers to the alcohol-induced impairment of driving skills. The rate of fatal crashes among drinking drivers under age 21 is more than twice the rate for those 21 and older.

Suicide. Alcohol use interacts with conditions such as depression and stress to contribute to suicide, the third leading cause of death among people between the ages of 14 and 25. In one study, 37 percent of eighth grade females who drank heavily reported attempting suicide, compared with 11 percent who did not drink.

Sexual Assault. Sexual assault, including rape, occurs most commonly among women in late adolescence and early adulthood, usually within the context of a date. In one survey, approximately 10 percent of female high school students reported having been raped. Research suggests that alcohol use by the offender, the victim, or both, increases the likelihood of sexual assault by a male acquaintance.

High-Risk Sex. Research has associated adolescent alcohol use with high-risk sex (for example, having multiple sexual partners, failing to use condoms, and having unplanned sex). The consequences of high-risk sex also are common in this age group, particularly unwanted pregnancy and sexually transmitted diseases, including HIV/AIDS. According to a recent study, the link between high-risk sex and drinking is affected by the quantity of alcohol consumed. The probability of sexual intercourse is increased by drinking amounts of alcohol sufficient to impair judgment, but decreased by drinking heavier amounts that result in feelings of nausea, passing out, or mental confusion.

Lasting Consequences

Adolescence is the transition between childhood and adulthood. During this time, significant changes occur in the body, including rapid hormonal alterations and the formation of new networks in the brain. Adolescence also is a time of trying new things and, especially, conforming to peer-group standards. These new activities may place young people at particular risk for experimenting with alcohol and continuing to drink. Exposing the brain to alcohol during this period may interrupt key processes of brain development, possibly leading to subtle learning impairments as well as to further escalation of drinking.

People who begin drinking before age 15 are four times more likely to develop alcohol dependence at some time in their lives compared with those who have their first drink at age 20 or older. It is not clear whether starting to drink at an early age actually causes alcoholism or whether it simply indicates an existing vulnerability to alcohol use disorders. For example, both early drinking and alcoholism had been linked to personality characteristics such as strong tendencies to act impulsively and to seek out new experiences and sensations. Some evidence indicates that genetic factors may contribute to the relationship between early drinking and subsequent alcoholism. Environmental factors also may be involved, especially in alcoholic families, where children may start drinking earlier because of easier access to alcohol in the home, family acceptance of drinking, and lack of parental monitoring.

Prevention and Treatment

Effective prevention and treatment programs are vital to reduce the risks associated with adolescent alcohol use. Research on the factors that contribute to the initiation and escalation of drinking is essential for the development of such programs. It should be noted that preventing and identifying alcohol use disorders in youth require different screening, assessment, and treatment approaches than those used for adults. For example, although relapse rates following alcoholism treatment are similar for both adults and adolescents, social factors such as peer pressure play a much larger role in relapse among adolescents.

Personal factors such as childhood behavior problems or a family history of alcohol use disorders can help to identify high-risk youth and may suggest directions for interventions. Perhaps the most reliable predictor of a youth's drinking behavior is the drinking behavior of his or her friends.

Most adolescents overestimate how much their peers drink and how positive their peers' attitudes are toward drinking. Many prevention programs help dispel these myths about peers' drinking practices.

Family factors, such as parent-child relationships, discipline methods, communication, monitoring and supervision, and parental involvement, also exert a significant influence on youthful alcohol use. Accordingly, family-based prevention programs for youth have been developed, which have significantly delayed initiation of alcohol use by improving parenting skills and family bonding.

Some school-based programs are aimed at adolescents who have already begun drinking. Preliminary research also has found promise in high school–based motivational programs that encourage self-change in problem drinkers.

Policy and Community Strategies

Another important factor in underage drinking is availability, that is, how easy it is for an underage drinker to obtain alcohol. Interventions aimed at the individual must be supplemented by policy changes to help reduce youth access to alcohol and decrease the harmful consequences of established drinking. For example, raising the minimum legal drinking age in all States to 21 saved an estimated 20,000 lives between 1975 and 2000. In addition, all States now have zero-tolerance laws, which set the legal blood alcohol limit for drivers younger than age 21 at 0.00 or 0.02 percent. These lower blood alcohol limits for young drivers have been associated with a 20-percent decline in the proportion of single-vehicle, nighttime fatal crashes among drivers younger than age 21.

Another successful prevention strategy uses simple fear of punishment to deter drinking and driving. That is, increased enforcement of laws to stop driving under the influence (DUI), coupled with increased media attention on those enforcement tactics, increases people's perception that they will be caught if they drink and drive, making them less likely to drive while under the influence.

The most successful interventions will draw on family, school, and community components to prevent or reduce alcohol use among adolescents. Project Northland is one such promising program. This intervention was initiated in a group of sixth graders. By the eighth grade, these students were less likely to use alcohol, especially the students who had not yet started drinking when the program began. Project Northland activities were resumed in grades 11 and 12 and had a significant positive effect on the students' tendency to avoid alcohol use and binge drinking. Taken together, the results show the effectiveness of continued, age-appropriate prevention activities for delaying or reducing underage drinking.

NIAAA Takes the Lead to Stop Underage Drinking

The immediate and long-term risks associated with adolescent alcohol use underscore the need for effective prevention and treatment programs. Research toward these ends is a top priority at NIAAA.

Through prevention and intervention strategies directed at the individual, family, school, and community, NIAAA seeks to increase public awareness of alcohol's effects and to reinforce the message that underage drinking is unacceptable, illegal, and dangerous.

Intervention tools such as Project Northland have shown promise in curbing underage alcohol use. Additional studies that follow groups of young people from childhood through their college years, at different locations and in different settings, will help determine whether interventions such as these are enduring and broadly applicable. Finding lasting solutions to the problem of underage drinking will be difficult; diligent research efforts offer the best hope for meeting this urgent challenge.

CHAPTER 2

Patterns of Teenage Alcohol Consumption

Perceptions and Misperceptions About Alcohol Consumption

Office of Juvenile Justice and Delinquency Prevention (OJJDP)

The Office of Juvenile Justice and Delinquency Prevention (OJJDP) is a federal government bureau that supports states and communities in the implementation of prevention and intervention programs related to juvenile delinquency. The following report summarizes alcohol consumption trends in the United States, observing that the vast majority of adults either abstain from drinking alcohol or drink on rare occasions. The report also compares adult and youth drinking patterns, determining that teenage alcohol drinkers are more likely to engage in risky behaviors such as binge drinking. Current public policies that endorse moderate drinking, the report contends, do not adequately address the problems associated with heavy adult and youth drinking. The authors recommend alternative strategies to address binge drinking, including increasing alcohol prices, restricting alcohol outlets, strengthening and enforcing minimum-age laws, holding adults who provide alcohol to minors accountable, and controlling alcohol advertising. Given that most adults abstain or rarely drink alcohol, the report maintains, a stricter alcohol policy will have little impact on the majority of Americans; however, such a policy will likely reduce the number of serious drinking problems, particularly among young people.

Myths About American Drinking

"Alcohol is an integral part of American life. It is a normal accompaniment to most social events. Most Americans enjoy drinking on a regular basis." These are widely held perceptions

Office of Juvenile Justice and Delinquency Prevention (OJJDP), "Drinking in America: Myths, Realities, and Prevention Policy," 2002. Reproduced by permission.

about alcohol—created in part by alcohol advertising and popular culture. But these perceptions are not entirely true. These perceptions—and misperceptions—affect our attitudes toward alcohol and our policies regarding the sale to and consumption of alcohol by youth as well as adults.

This paper provides a more realistic picture of who drinks, how much, and how often. It compares the drinking patterns of adults to those of people under age 21. It then analyzes the implications of these drinking patterns for alcohol policy.

Alcohol: Counting the Cost

While there are many positive impressions associated with alcohol, Americans are becoming conscious of the problems created by alcohol. For example, we no longer accept impaired-driving crashes as unavoidable "accidents." But alcohol-related problems go well beyond impaired driving. In fact, more than 75,000 deaths are attributable to alcohol consumption each year and the economic costs associated with alcohol problems total more than $184 billion annually. As large as they are, these figures do not begin to capture all of alcohol's social and health toll; more than one-third of Americans report that alcohol has caused problems in their immediate family.

When society views drinking as a normal and accepted part of life, these problems may seem inevitable. Some of this view is based on misperception of drinking patterns. A more accurate picture has implications for strategies to reduce alcohol-related problems.

Adults: Who Drinks and How Much?

A large majority of Americans either do not drink or drink infrequently. For this majority alcohol is an unimportant consumer product. According to the National Survey on Drug Use and Health (an interview survey carried out in homes), about 46 percent of adults 21 years of age and older report that they did not consume any alcohol in the past month and an additional 26 percent report drinking once a week or less.

In addition to information about how frequently people drink, it is also important to examine the quantity people typically drink on each occasion. . . . Among adults, 46 percent did not drink at all, and 31 percent drank but did not have five or more drinks on any occasion. That is, 77 percent of adults do not drink at a hazardous level.

Even among drinkers, only a minority consume this much alcohol on any occasion. About 43 percent of adult drinkers had five or more drinks on any occasion in the last 30 days.

The average number of drinks consumed by drinkers who do not binge was fewer than three per week. By contrast, frequent bingers who have had five or more drinks at a time five or more times in the past month consume on average more than 24 drinks per week. Even though frequent bingers are only seven percent of the population, they drink 45 percent of the alcohol consumed by adults in the United States. . . .

- Binge drinkers are 23 percent of the population, but drink 76 percent of the alcohol.

- Frequent bingers are only 7 percent of the population, but drink 45 percent of the alcohol.

These statistics show the importance of heavy drinkers for the alcohol market. Alcohol sales depend on the heaviest drinking consumers. The claim that the "overwhelming majority of Americans" use alcohol responsibly is true only because most Americans either abstain or consume alcohol very infrequently.

The following picture of adult drinking emerges from these data:

- Most American adults either abstain or drink very little.

- A relatively small percentage of drinkers drink most of the alcohol.

- This small percentage often consumes several drinks at a time, increasing the risk of serious health and safety problems.

Underage: Who Drinks and How Much?

The picture for underage drinking is somewhat different. Most young people reported to the National Household Survey that they had not had anything to drink in the last month. About 94 percent of 12- to 14-year-olds reported that they had not drunk alcohol while 72 percent of 15- to 17-year-olds and 49 percent of 18- to 20-year-olds reported that they had not drunk in the preceding month. . . .

In terms of the quantity of drinking, the proportion of young drinkers who report drinking heavily (five or more drinks at a sitting) is higher than for adults.

While about 43 percent of adult drinkers report heavy drinking on one or more occasions in the past month, 50 percent of 12- to 14-year-old drinkers, 65 percent of 15- to 17-year-old drinkers and 72 percent of 18- to 20-year-old drinkers report heavy drinking in the past month.

Young people who drink heavily consume the vast majority of the alcohol consumed by their age group. Percentages range from 91 percent for 12- to 14-year-olds to 96 percent for 18- to 20-year-olds. Underage drinkers consume about 11 percent of all the alcohol purchased in the United States in 2002, and the vast majority of this alcohol is consumed in a risky fashion.

The following picture of underage drinking emerges:

- The majority of young people abstain from regular use of alcohol—a greater percentage than adults.

- Young people who do consume alcohol are more likely than adults to drink heavily.

- The small proportion of youth who drink heavily consume the vast majority of the alcohol consumed by underage drinkers.

Social Norms and Social Policy: Correcting Perceptions

How do social beliefs about drinking affect our efforts to prevent problems associated with drinking? Social norms and expectations play a powerful role in shaping the *alcohol environment* at both the community and societal level. The belief that most adults drink in moderate amounts without problems translates into public policies that make alcohol readily available at low prices and permit widespread marketing that communicates only positive messages about alcohol's effects. These policies in turn create an environment that encourages alcohol use and downplays its potential for harm to public health and safety.

Although we may think that our alcohol policies are simply helping to meet the demand from moderate-drinking adults, they are actually accommodating heavy and hazardous drinking by a small minority of consumers, many of whom are underage. Such policies undercut our efforts to reduce alcohol-related problems and underage drinking.

Consider the impact of the following environmental influences on potential consumers—especially young people.

- *Alcohol is cheap and becoming cheaper.* The real price of alcohol has been steadily dropping for the last five decades, in part due to the decline in the real value of alcohol excise taxes (which have been eroded by inflation). Cheap beers are now roughly the same price as popular brands of soft drinks. Price promotions, such as happy hours and drinking games, often target young drinkers and promote binge drinking.

- *Americans are bombarded with $4 billion of alcohol marketing each year.* Alcohol advertising and product placements are very common and often occur on television and in radio shows for which the majority of the audience is underage, on Internet sites attractive to young people, and on billboards and in retail outlets where young people are frequently present. Advertising often uses youth-oriented themes.

- *Alcohol is one of the most readily available consumer products.* Many communities, especially in low-income areas, are saturated with alcohol outlets. Alcohol is often more available than basic staples and school supplies. Alcohol sales are often key to the success of convenience stores and gas stations, which may be located in residential areas, near schools, and in other locations frequented by children.

- *New alcohol products cater to youthful tastes and may promote underage drinking.* Sweet alcohol products blur the line between alcohol and soft drinks; malt liquors, which have high alcohol content and low prices, are sold in 40-ounce and larger containers used by young people as single servings. Clever marketing ploys—such as test tube "shots," containers that look like TNT explosives, and drinks that change the color of the drinker's tongue—target youthful drinkers.

Our community environments make alcohol easily available and send messages that promote alcohol's glamour and attractiveness.

Realistic Perceptions: Effective Policies

The common public perception is that the majority of people drink alcohol and that most alcohol is consumed in a moderate fashion. Given these perceptions, the public and policy makers are often reluctant to impose restrictions and controls on how alcohol is manufactured, promoted, sold, and consumed; if the vast majority of adults drink responsibly, then controls on sales place a burden on these responsible drinkers.

However, most Americans do not drink frequently and most alcohol is consumed by heavy drinkers and in a risky fashion. Therefore, controls on alcohol have little or no impact on the majority of Americans, but such controls *can* reduce heavy and hazardous drinking, especially among underage drinkers.

A variety of policies have been proven to be effective or show promise in reducing alcohol consumption and related problems. Some key policy strategies are discussed briefly in the section that follows.

Increasing Alcohol Prices

Alcohol prices have not kept pace with inflation, and thus, the real price of alcohol has been dropping steadily. Many different studies have found that higher alcohol prices lead to lower consumption and fewer alcohol-related problems. Higher prices tend to have a particularly strong effect on young people.

One common argument made against increases in alcohol prices is that such price increases would penalize the majority of responsible drinkers. As has been shown here, the vast majority of Americans would feel little or no impact from a price increase because they do not drink or drink very little and infrequently.

Restricting Alcohol Outlets

Restricting the density of alcohol outlets and their location is one way of decreasing consumption and related problems. Several studies have demonstrated the connection between the density of alcohol outlets in a community and the rates of violence, particularly among youth. Alcohol outlets can be restricted through limiting the number or density of outlets or through limiting the types of locations where alcohol may be sold. For example, many communities have imposed limits on sales or consumption of alcohol in public places (such as parks and beaches), at public events (such as fairs and festivals), or at certain kinds of retail locations (such as gas stations).

Strengthening and Enforcing Minimum Purchase Age Laws

Raising the minimum purchase age for alcohol has been very effective in reducing drinking and related problems among young people. Despite the progress that has been made, young people report that alcohol is readily available from a variety of sources, in part because current laws are not well enforced. Effective enforcement of the law can substantially reduce youth alcohol access. In addition, strengthening existing laws to further restrict youth access to alcohol shows promise in reducing underage drinking and related problems. For example, some communities require that purchasers of kegs of beer be registered in order to deter serving keg beer to underage drinkers at parties.

Strategies Aimed at Curbing Social Availability

Young people can obtain alcohol from noncommercial sources such as older friends, family members and other adults who buy or provide alcohol to them. Adults who provide alcohol to minors can be held accountable for their actions through enforcement and policy approaches aimed at social availability of alcohol. Shoulder tap operations focus on third-party transactions of alcohol that involve adults purchasing alcohol for youth. Social host liability laws and proactive party patrols and controlled party dispersal operations may also deter adults from hosting underage parties and providing alcohol to minors.

Controlling Alcohol Advertising and Promotion

Studies on the effects of advertising on adults do not show a strong connection between exposure to advertising and overall consumption. However, survey studies on alcohol advertising and young people consistently indicate that children and adolescents who are exposed to alcohol advertisements have more favorable attitudes toward drinking, are more likely to be underage drinkers, and intend to drink more when they are adults. The fact that these survey effects are small may be due, in part, to the pervasiveness of alcohol advertising in the environment. Nearly everyone is exposed to hundreds or even thousands of alcohol advertisements each year. It is impossible to say what effect a major change in the nature of the alcohol messages in the environment might have.

Public Support for Alcohol Policy Change

It is often believed that moderate drinking Americans would not support policies that would make alcohol more expensive or more inconvenient to obtain. After all, we believe the status quo reflects what people want. A recent survey of public opinion, however, demonstrates that these assumptions are inaccurate. There is strong public support for policies designed to create a healthier environment with regard to alcohol, especially to prevent alcohol problems among youth. These survey findings shouldn't be surprising—after all, most people have no stake at all in the current status quo that makes alcohol so readily available and attractive because they either do not drink or drink very little and infrequently.

[Below are] . . . some of the findings from the *Youth Access to Alcohol Survey* published in September 1998.

Large majorities of the population favor various regulatory strategies designed to reduce underage drinking problems, including such things as

- alcohol tax increases to pay for prevention programs

- restrictions on alcohol advertising to make drinking less appealing to young people

- compliance check programs (in which law enforcement agencies use underage decoys to determine whether alcohol retailers are selling to minors)

- keg registration laws to deter the purchase of kegs of beer for underage consumption

- restrictions on public drinking in locations where young people are likely to be present.

Strict Policies Reduce Drinking Problems

Most Americans either abstain from alcohol or drink very infrequently—less than once a week. Our public policies and social norms, however, do not reflect this fact and make alcohol readily accessible at low prices. Alcohol sales are dominated by a relatively small minority of the population who drink heavily. Policies and norms that promote alcohol availability support and encourage these problematic drinking behaviors. Most Americans consume very little alcohol, so it is not surprising that large majorities of the population support stricter alcohol policies designed to reduce drinking problems, especially among young people. These policy reforms have been shown to be effective in reducing alcohol consumption and problems.

Parents Who Allow Underage Drinking Send Kids the Wrong Message

About.com

The following report issued by the American Medical Association (AMA) presents the results of two polls taken by teenagers and parents, in which the respondents express their opinions about the accessibility of alcohol to minors and those who typically supply it to them. Perhaps the most surprising statistic comes from the teen survey, the report contends, in which respondents indicated that their own parents often supplied them with alcohol. In fact, nearly 25 percent of adolescents, aged thirteen to eighteen, and some 33 percent of girls, aged sixteen to eighteen, state that their own parents have given them alcohol. Viewing underage drinking as a serious public health threat, the AMA urges physicians to take an active role in advising parents about the risks of providing alcohol to minors.

Parents' Attitude 'Of Great Concern,' AMA Says

A survey by the American Medical Association [AMA] shows that underage youth obtain alcohol easily and often and many times the source of their alcohol is their own parents.

The polls also show parental opinions and behaviors about providing alcohol to teenagers and perceptions on how youth acquire alcohol.

"From a public health standpoint, these findings are frankly disturbing," said J. Edward Hill, M.D., president of the AMA. "While it is of great concern to see how easily teens, especially young girls, get alcohol, it is alarming to know that legal-age adults, even parents, are supplying the alcohol."

The poll of teens, aged 13–18, found that nearly half reported having obtained alcohol at some point. In all age groups, girls nearly always ranked higher than boys in obtaining alcohol.

In the adult poll, about one out of four U.S. parents with children, aged 12–20 (26 percent), agree that teens should be able to drink at home with their parents present.

"Policies and law enforcement efforts to stop minors from obtaining alcohol are important, but this data reveals how easily avoided those policies and laws can be when legal-aged buyers are the leading source of alcohol for children," said Hill. "And even parents who do not buy for their children could be unwitting sources if their alcohol at home is left unsecured."

Two out of three teens, aged 13–18, said it is easy to get alcohol from their homes without parents knowing about it. One third responded that it is easy to obtain alcohol from their own parents knowingly, which increases to 40 percent when it is from a friend's parent. And one in four teens have attended a party where minors were drinking in front of parents.

"Parents allowing underage children to drink under their supervision are under a dangerous misperception," said Hill. "Injuries and car accidents after such parent-hosted parties remind us that no parent can completely control the actions of intoxicated youth, during or after a party. And the main message children hear is that drinking illegally is okay."

Parents Supplied Alcohol

The polls were funded as part of the AMA's partnership with The Robert Wood Johnson Foundation. Other key findings of the two polls include:

- Nearly one in four teens, aged 13–18, and one in three girls, aged 16–18, say their own parents have supplied them with alcohol, and teens who have obtained alcohol reported that, in the past six months, parents were the suppliers three times on average.

- While 71 percent of parents with children, aged 12–20, disagreed with the statement that teen drinking was okay if a parent were present, 76 percent think it is likely that teenagers get alcohol from someone's parent—and they knew about it.

- One out of four parents of children, aged 12–20 (25 percent), say they have allowed their teens to drink with their supervision in the past six months. Approximately one in 12 (8 percent) indicated they have allowed their teen's friends to also drink under their supervision in the past six months.

- While only eight percent of parents of children aged 12–20 indicated that they allowed their teen and his/her friends to drink with supervision in the past six months, 21 percent of teens attended a party where the alcohol was provided by someone else's parents. And 27 percent of teens attended a party where youth were drinking with parents present. This discrepancy suggests parents are unaware that other parents are allowing their own children to drink.

"The AMA applauds parents who discourage and disallow underage drinking," said Hill. "We hope that such parents willing to stand up for their children's health will be more vocal in their communities, letting children and other parents know that no adult should substitute their judgment for a teen's own parents. Drinking is not a rite of passage. Fatal car accidents, injuries and assaults, and irreversible damage to the brain are not rites of passage for any child."

Alcohol Is Everywhere

The AMA said the poll results underscore the need for physicians to counsel parents on the health risks of alcohol use, as well as to advocate for policies to restrict access to minors. To assist physicians in their efforts, the AMA unveiled an informational poster for use in physician offices. The poster is the second in a series of educational materials that will help start a dialogue on this important health issue.

"Alcohol is everywhere," said Steven Harris, a 14-year-old from San Bruno, California. "Young people see ads everywhere. We see drinking on TV and in the movies, and we see it at parties and at home. And it is probably harder for teens to get into an R-rated movie than to get alcohol. It's a joke."

Teenage Alcohol Abuse Creates a Vast Public Health Problem

National Institute on Alchohol Abuse and Alcoholism (NIAAA)

The National Institute on Alchohol Abuse and Alcoholism (NIAAA) is a component of the National Institutes of Health within the U.S. Department of Health and Human Services (HHS), a federal government agency committed to protecting the well-being of all Americans. The HHS sponsor more than three hundred programs that address all aspects of health care. In the following report, the NIAAA characterizes underage drinking as a leading public health issue in the United States. The report discusses the various reasons why adolescents may choose to drink, including the thrill of engaging in risky behavior, a greater sensitivity to the positive effects of drinking, and hereditary and environmental factors. The report also surveys scientific research on the harmful long-term health problems associated with underage drinking and proposes that perhaps the most effective way to combat the problem is to evaluate each particular adolescent's "whole system" of development, including physical, genetic, psychological, social, and environmental factors. The study concludes with a discussion of environmental and individual-oriented intervention programs, weighing their relative successes and failures.

Alcohol is the drug of choice among youth. Many young people are experiencing the consequences of drinking too much, at too early age. As a result, underage drinking is a leading public health problem in this country.

Each year, approximately 5,000 young people under the age of 21 die as a result of underage drinking; this includes

National Institute on Alchohol Abuse and Alcoholism (NIAAA), "Underage Drinking: Why Do Adolescents Drink, What Are the Risks, and How Can Underage Drinking Be Prevented?" U.S. Department of Health & Human Services, January 2006.

about 1,900 deaths from motor vehicle crashes, 1,600 as a result of homicides, 300 from suicide, as well as hundreds from other injuries such as falls, burns, and drownings.

Yet drinking continues to be widespread among adolescents, as shown by nationwide surveys as well as studies in smaller populations. According to data from the 2005 Monitoring the Future (MTF) study, an annual survey of U.S. youth, three-fourths of 12th graders, more than two-thirds of 10th graders, and about two in every five 8th graders have consumed alcohol. And when youth drink they tend to drink intensively, often consuming four to five drinks at one time. MTF data show that 11 percent of 8th graders, 22 percent of 10th graders, and 29 percent of 12th graders had engaged in heavy episodic (or "binge") drinking within the past two weeks.

Research also shows that many adolescents start to drink at very young ages. In 2003, the average age of first use of alcohol was about 14, compared to about 17 ½ in 1965. People who reported starting to drink before the age of 15 were four times more likely to also report meeting the criteria for alcohol dependence at some point in their lives. In fact, new research shows that the serious drinking problems (including what is called alcoholism) typically associated with middle age actually begin to appear much earlier, during young adulthood and even adolescence.

Other research shows that the younger children and adolescents are when they start to drink, the more likely they will be to engage in behaviors that harm themselves and others. For example, frequent binge drinkers (nearly 1 million high school students nationwide) are more likely to engage in risky behaviors, including using other drugs such as marijuana and cocaine, having sex with six or more partners, and earning grades that are mostly Ds and Fs in school.

Why Do Some Adolescents Drink?

As children move from adolescence to young adulthood, they encounter dramatic physical, emotional, and lifestyle changes. Developmental transitions, such as puberty and increasing independence, have been associated with alcohol use. So in a sense, just being an adolescent may be a key risk factor not only starting to drink but also for drinking dangerously.

Risk-Taking—Research shows the brain keeps developing well into the twenties, during which time it continues to establish important communication connections and further refines its function. Scientists believe that this lengthy developmental period may help explain some of the behavior which is characteristic of adolescence—such as their propensity to seek out new and potentially dangerous situations. For some teens, thrill-seeking might include experimenting with alcohol. Developmental changes also offer a possible physiological explanation for why teens act so impulsively, often not recognizing that their actions—such as drinking—have consequences.

Expectancies—How people view alcohol and its effects also influences their drinking behavior, including whether they begin to drink and how much. An adolescent who expects drinking to be a pleasurable experience is more likely to drink than one who does not. An important area of alcohol research is focusing on how expectancy influences drinking patterns from childhood through adolescence and into young adulthood. Beliefs about alcohol are established very early in life, even before the child begins elementary school. Before age 9, children generally view alcohol negatively and see drinking as bad, with adverse effects. By about age 13, however, their expectancies shift, becoming more positive. As would be expected, adolescents who drink the most also place the greatest emphasis on the positive and arousing effects of alcohol.

Sensitivity and Tolerance to Alcohol—Differences between the adult brain and the brain of the maturing adolescent also may help to explain why many young drinkers are able to consume much larger amounts of alcohol than adults before experiencing the negative consequences of drinking, such as drowsiness, lack of coordination, and withdrawal/hangover effects. This unusual tolerance may help to explain the high rates of binge drinking among young adults. At the same time, adolescents appear to be particularly sensitive to the positive effects of drinking, such as feeling more at ease in social situations, and young people may drink more than adults because of these positive social experiences.

Personality Characteristics and Psychiatric Comorbidity—Children who begin to drink at a very early age (before age 12) often share similar personality characteristics that may make them more likely to start drinking. Young people who are disruptive, hyperactive, and aggressive—often referred to as having conduct problems or being antisocial—as well as those who are depressed, withdrawn, or anxious, may be at greatest risk for alcohol problems. Other behavior problems associated with alcohol use include rebelliousness, difficulty avoiding harm or harmful situations, and a host of other traits seen in young people who act out without regard for rules or the feelings of others (i.e., disinhibition).

Hereditary Factors—Some of the behavior and physiological factors that converge to increase or decrease a person's risk for alcohol problems, including tolerance to alcohol's effects, may be directly linked to genetics. For example, being a child of an alcoholic or having several alcoholic family members places a person at greater risk for alcohol problems. Children of alcoholics (COAs) are between 4 and 10 times more likely to become alcoholics themselves than are children who have no close relatives with alcoholism. COAs also are more likely to begin drinking at a young age and to progress to drinking problems more quickly.

Research shows that COAs may have subtle brain differences which could be markers for developing later alcohol problems. For example, using high-tech brain-imaging techniques, scientists have found that COAs have a distinctive feature in one brainwave pattern (called a P300 response) that could be a marker for later alcoholism risk. Researchers also are investigating other brainwave differences in COAs that may be present long before they begin to drink, including brainwave activity recorded during sleep, as well as changes in brain structure and function.

Some studies suggest that these brain differences may be particularly evident in people who also have certain behavioral traits, such as signs of conduct disorder, antisocial personality disorder, sensation-seeking, or poor impulse control. Studying how the brain's structure and function translates to behavior will help researchers to better understand how pre-drinking risk factors shape later alcohol use. For example, does a person who is depressed drink to alleviate his or her depression, or does drinking lead to changes in his brain that result in feelings of depression?

Other hereditary factors likely will become evident as scientists work to identify the actual genes involved in addiction. By analyzing the genetic makeup of people and families with alcohol dependence, researchers have found specific regions on chromosomes that correlate with a risk for alcoholism. Candidate genes for alcoholism risk also have been associated with those regions. The goal now is to further refine regions for which a specific gene has not yet been identified and then determine how those genes interact with other genes and gene products as well as with the environment to result in alcohol dependence. Further research also should shed light on the extent to which the same or different genes contribute to alcohol problems, both in adults and in adolescents.

Environmental Aspects—Pinpointing a genetic contribution will not tell the whole story, however, as drinking behavior reflects a complex interplay between inherited and environmental factors, the implications of which are only beginning to be explored in adolescents. And what influences drinking at one age may not have the same impact at another. As [R.J.] Rose and colleagues show, genetic factors appear to have more influence on adolescent drinking behavior in late adolescence than in mid-adolescence.

Environmental factors, such as the influence of parents and peers, also play a role in alcohol use. For example, parents who drink more and who view drinking favorably may have children who drink more, and an adolescent girl with an older or adult boyfriend is more likely to use alcohol and other drugs and to engage in delinquent behaviors.

Researchers are examining other environmental influences as well, such as the impact of the media. Today alcohol is widely available and aggressively promoted through television, radio, billboards, and the Internet. Researchers are studying how young people react to these advertisements. In a study of 3rd, 6th, and 9th graders, those who found alcohol ads desirable were more likely to view drinking positively and to want to purchase products with alcohol logos. Research is mixed, however, on whether these positive views of alcohol actually lead to underage drinking.

What Are the Health Risks?

Whatever it is that leads adolescents to begin drinking, once they start they face a number of potential health risks. Although the severe health problems associated with harmful alcohol use are not as common in adolescents as they are in adults, studies show that young people who drink heavily may put themselves at risk for a range of potential health problems.

Brain Effects—Scientists currently are examining just how alcohol affects the developing brain, but it's a difficult task. Subtle changes in the brain may be difficult to detect but still have a significant impact on long-term thinking and memory skills. Add to this the fact that adolescent brains are still maturing, and the study of alcohol's effects becomes even more complex. Research has shown that animals fed alcohol during this critical developmental stage continue to show long-lasting impairment from alcohol as they age. It's simply not known how alcohol will affect the long-term memory and learning skills of people who began drinking heavily as adolescents.

Liver Effects—Elevated liver enzymes, indicating some degree of liver damage, have been found in some adolescents who drink alcohol. Young drinkers who are overweight or obese showed elevated liver enzymes even with only moderate levels of drinking.

Growth and Endocrine Effects—In both males and females, puberty is a period associated with marked hormonal changes, including increases in the sex hormones, estrogen and testosterone. These hormones, in turn, increase production of other hormones and growth factors, which are vital for normal organ development. Drinking alcohol during this period of rapid growth and development (i.e., prior to or during puberty) may upset the critical hormonal balance necessary for normal development of organs, muscles, and bones. Studies in animals also show that consuming alcohol during puberty adversely affects the maturation of the reproductive system.

Preventing Underage Drinking Within a Developmental Framework

Complex behaviors, such as the decision to begin drinking or to continue using alcohol, are the result of a dynamic interplay between genes and environment. For example, biological and physiological changes that occur during adolescence may promote risk-taking behavior, leading to early experimentation with alcohol. This behavior then shapes the child's environment, as he or she chooses friends and situations that support further drinking. Continued drinking may lead to physiological reactions, such as depression or anxiety disorders, triggering even greater alcohol use or dependence. In this way, youthful patterns of alcohol use can mark the start of a developmental pathway that may lead to abuse and dependence. Then again, not all young people who travel this pathway experience the same outcomes.

Perhaps the best way to understand and prevent underage alcohol use is to view drinking as it relates to development. This "whole system" approach to underage drinking takes into account a particular adolescent's unique risk and protective factors—from genetics and personality characteristics to social and environmental factors. Viewed in this way, development includes not only the adolescent's inherent risk and resilience but also the current conditions that help to shape his or her behavior.

Children mature at different rates. Developmental research takes this into account, recognizing that during adolescence there are periods of rapid growth and reorganization, alternating with periods of slower growth and integration of body systems. Periods of rapid transitions, when social or cultural factors most strongly influence the biology and behavior of the adolescent, may be the best time to target delivery of interventions. Interventions that focus on these critical development periods could alter the life course of the child, perhaps placing him or her on a path to avoid problems with alcohol.

To date, researchers have been unable to identify a single track that predicts the course of alcohol use for all or even most young people. Instead, findings provide strong evidence for wide developmental variation in drinking patterns within this special population.

Interventions for Preventing Underage Drinking

Intervention approaches typically fall into two distinct categories: (1) environmental-level interventions, which seek to reduce opportunities for underage drinking, increase penalties for violating minimum legal drinking age (MLDA) and other alcohol use laws, and reduce community tolerance for alcohol use by youth; and (2) individual-level interventions, which seek to change knowledge, expectancies, attitudes, intentions, motivation, and skills so that youth are better able to resist the pro-drinking influences and opportunities that surround them.

Environmental approaches include:

Raising the Price of Alcohol—A substantial body of research has shown that higher prices or taxes on alcoholic beverages are associated with lower levels of alcohol consumption and alcohol-related problems, especially in young people.

Increasing the Minimum Legal Drinking Age—Today all States have set the minimum legal drinking at age 21. Increasing the age at which people can legally purchase and drink alcohol has been the most successful intervention to date in reducing drinking and alcohol-related crashes among people under age 21. NHTSA [National Highway Traffic Safety Administration] estimates that a legal drinking age of 21 saves 700 to 1,000 lives annually. Since 1976, these laws have prevented more than 21,000 traffic deaths. Just how much the legal drinking age relates to drinking-related crashes is shown by a recent study in New Zealand. Six years ago [2000] that country lowered its minimum legal drinking age to 18. Since then, alcohol-related crashes have risen 12 percent among 18- to 19-year-olds and 14 percent among 15- to 17-year-olds. Clearly a higher minimum drinking age can help to reduce crashes and save lives, especially in very young drivers.

Enacting Zero-Tolerance Laws—All States have zero-tolerance laws that make it illegal for people under age 21 to drive after *any* drinking. When the first eight States to adopt zero-tolerance laws were compared with nearby States without such laws, the zero-tolerance States showed a 21-percent greater decline in the proportion of single-vehicle night-time fatal crashes involving drivers under 21, the type of crash most likely to involve alcohol.

Stepping up Enforcement of Laws—Despite their demonstrated benefits, legal drinking age and zero-tolerance laws generally have not been vigorously enforced. Alcohol purchase laws aimed at sellers and buyers also can be effective, but resources must be made available for enforcing these laws.

Individual-focused interventions include:

School-Based Prevention Programs—The first school-based prevention programs were primarily informational and often used scare tactics; it was assumed that if youth understood the dangers of alcohol use, they would choose not to drink. These programs were ineffective. Today, better programs are available and often have a number of elements in common: They follow social influence models and include setting norms, addressing social pressures to drink, and teaching resistance skills. These programs also offer interactive and developmentally appropriate information, include peer-led components, and provide teacher training.

Family-Based Prevention Programs—Parents' ability to influence whether their children drink is well documented and is consistent across racial/ethnic groups. Setting clear rules against drinking, consistently enforcing those rules, and monitoring the child's behavior all help to reduce the likelihood of underage drinking. The Iowa Strengthening Families Program (ISFP), delivered when students were in grade 6, is a program that has shown long-lasting preventive effects on alcohol use.

Selected Programs Showing Promise

Environmental interventions are among the recommendations included in the recent National Research Council (NRC) and Institute of Medicine (IOM) report on underage drinking. These interventions are intended to reduce commercial and social availability of alcohol and/or reduce driving while intoxicated. They use a variety of strategies, including server training and compliance checks in places that sell alcohol; deterring adults from purchasing alcohol for minors or providing alcohol to minors; restricting drinking in public places and preventing underage drinking parties; enforcing penalties for the use of false IDs, driving while intoxicated, and violating zero-tolerance laws; and raising public awareness of policies and sanctions.

The following community trials show how environmental strategies can be useful in reducing underage drinking and related problems.

The Massachusetts Saving Lives Program—This intervention was designed to reduce alcohol-impaired driving and related traffic deaths. Strategies included the use of drunk driving checkpoints, speeding and drunk driving awareness days, speed-watch telephone hotlines, high school peer-led education, and college prevention programs. The 5-year program decreased fatal crashes, particularly alcohol-related fatal crashes involving drivers ages 15–25, and reduced the proportion of 16- to 19-year-olds who reported driving after drinking, in comparison with the rest of Massachusetts. It also made teens more aware of penalties for drunk driving and for speeding.

The Community Prevention Trial Program—This program was designed to reduce alcohol-involved injuries and death. One component sought to reduce alcohol sales to minors by enforcing underage sales laws; training sales clerks, owners, and managers to prevent sales of alcohol to minors; and using the media to raise community awareness of underage drinking. Sales to apparent minors (people of legal drinking age who appear younger than age 21) were significantly reduced in the intervention communities compared with control sites.

Communities Mobilizing for Change on Alcohol—This intervention, designed to reduce the accessibility of alcoholic beverages to people under age 21, centered on policy changes among local institutions to make underage drinking less acceptable within the community. Alcohol sales to minors were reduced: 18- to 20-year-olds were less likely to try to purchase alcohol or provide it to younger teens, and the number of DUI [driving under the influence] arrests declined among 18- to 20-year-olds.

Multicomponent Comprehensive Interventions—Perhaps the strongest approach for preventing underage drinking involves the coordinated effort of all the elements that influence a child's life—including family, schools, and community. Ideally, intervention programs also should integrate treatment for youth who are alcohol dependent. Project Northland is an example of a comprehensive program that has been extensively evaluated.

Project Northland was tested in 22 school districts in northeastern Minnesota. The intervention included (1) school curricula, (2) peer leadership, (3) parental involvement programs, and (4) communitywide task force activities to address larger community norms and alcohol availability. It targeted adolescents in grades 6 through 12.

Intervention and comparison communities differed significantly in "tendency to use alcohol," a composite measure that combined items about intentions to use alcohol and actual use as well as in the likelihood of drinking "five or more in a row." Underage drinking was less prevalent in the intervention communities during phase 1; higher during the interim period (suggesting a "catch-up" effect while intervention activities were minimal); and again lower during phase 2, when intervention activities resumed.

Project Northland has been designated a model program by the Substance Abuse and Mental Health Services Administration (SAMHSA), and its materials have been adapted for a general audience. It now is being replicated in ethnically diverse urban neighborhoods.

Prevention Programs Reduce Youth Experimentation

Today, alcohol is widely available and aggressively promoted throughout society. And alcohol use continues to be regarded, by many people, as a normal part of growing up. Yet underage drinking is dangerous, not only for the drinker but also for society, as evident by the number of alcohol-involved motor vehicle crashes, homicides, suicides, and other injuries.

People who begin drinking early in life run the risk of developing serious alcohol problems, including alcoholism, later in life. They also are at greater risk for a variety of adverse consequences, including risky sexual activity and poor performance in school.

Identifying adolescents at greatest risk can help stop problems before they develop. And innovative, comprehensive approaches to prevention, such as Project Northland, are showing success in reducing experimentation with alcohol as well as the problems that accompany alcohol use by young people.

Underage Drinking Takes a Heavy Toll on America's Kids

Susan Black

Susan Black reviews the findings of several scientific studies that examine the early age at which children begin drinking alcohol, the adverse social effects related to youth alcohol abuse, and the high incidence of mental disorders detected in alcohol-dependent adolescents. Posing the question of whether or not science can predict and therefore prevent alcohol abuse in teens, the author suggests that intervention programs should take into account the adolescents' individual risk factors and specific stages of development rather than focusing on a single factor that may contribute to alcohol dependence. One such program has been developed by the National Center on Addiction and Substance Abuse (CASA) at Columbia University, Black writes. Named CASASTART (Striving Together to Achieve Rewarding Tomorrows), this program uses a personalized approach aimed at preventing the first drink or first drug use by high-risk students aged eight to thirteen years old. Initial evaluations indicate that students in CASASTART were less likely to engage in destructive behavior, Black reports, while they were more likely to succeed in school when compared to a matched control group.

It took some sleuthing, but a middle school principal and a school police officer located a stash of vodka hidden by two eighth-grade boys. "The kids smuggled in one bottle at a time and concealed the liquor above the ceiling tiles in a second-story closet," the principal told me.

Confronted, the 13-year-olds admitted they often drank before classes and whenever they could sneak away unnoticed.

"These kids had their own private bar," the principal said, adding that the boys also sold swigs of alcohol to their friends.

In another middle school, a sixth-grade girl, addicted to alcohol after taking her first sip at a friend's slumber party, was placed in a residential treatment center. "At the beginning of the year," her school counselor said, "she was a pretty, bright, lively preteen, getting good grades and playing in the school orchestra. By midyear alcohol had almost destroyed her. Now she needs professional help to recover."

Are these cases of young drinkers the exception or the rule? Several recent studies on kids and alcohol show that drinking frequently begins at an early age, often before kids are officially teens. *Teens Today 2002*, a study conducted by SADD (Students Against Destructive Decisions/Students Against Driving Drunk) and Liberty Mutual Group, found that many kids take their first drink—and continue drinking—before they're 13.

The study, based on a national sample of more than 1,800 students, found that a first spike in alcohol use occurs between sixth and seventh grade, and a second spike follows between eighth and ninth grade. By 12th grade, more than three-quarters of teens in school drink alcohol—some occasionally, some frequently, and others on binges. Add dropouts to the mix, and the number of underage kids using alcohol soars even higher.

A Terrible Trajectory

Early drinking takes a heavy toll, as researchers at RAND's Drug Policy Research Center found when they followed some 3,400 seventh-grade students in 30 California and Oregon schools to age 23. As they report in the May 2003 issue of *Pediatrics*, 46 percent of seventh-graders in their study were experimenters who used alcohol infrequently; 31 percent were drinkers who consumed alcohol fairly regularly; and 23 percent were nondrinkers who abstained from taking a first drink.

The RAND researchers predict trouble-filled trajectories for kids who begin drinking by seventh grade. Young drinkers are more likely to have academic and social problems in school and problems of drug abuse and criminal behavior by their mid-20s. Compared to nondrinkers, these kids are far more likely to steal, be suspended, drop out of school, and engage in violent behavior.

In fact, early onset drinking is a "powerful predictor" of lifetime alcohol abuse and dependence, according to the National Institute on Alcohol Abuse and Alcoholism [NIAAA]. Bridget Grant, NIAAA's Chief of biometry and epidemiology, found in an institute study that more than 40 percent of youth who began drinking before age 13 are classified as alcohol dependent at some point in their lives. Young drinkers often end up coping with teen pregnancies and sexually transmitted diseases, and many succumb to depression and suicide. Postponing the onset of drinking to at least age 18, she says, sharply reduces these alcohol-related problems.

More evidence of early drinking dangers comes from studies conducted by psychologist Matt McGue and his co-researchers at the University of Minnesota. In a 2001 report published in *Alcoholism: Clinical & Experimental Research*, McGue says kids who take their first drink before age 15 are at risk for low achievement, delinquent and antisocial behavior, drug abuse, and alcoholism.

Often, he points out, early alcohol use is a symptom of existing problems or underlying vulnerability—and an inability or unwillingness to inhibit behaviors that result in negative consequences. Examples of behaviors associated with early onset drinking include conduct disorders, impulsivity, and refusal to accept and adhere to rules, regulations, and common societal norms.

The Psychological Connection

These findings are underscored by researchers from the University of Pittsburgh's School of Medicine. In a study for the

Pittsburgh Adolescent Alcohol Research Center, Duncan Clark and Oscar Bukstein found that 89 percent of alcohol-dependent teens also had a mental disorder, such as antisocial disorder (characterized by aggression, destruction of property, deceitfulness, theft, and violation of rules) or negative-affect disorder (characterized by severe bouts of depression).

Psychological problems and alcohol use among teens may be "indirectly linked by shared risk factors," these researchers say. In other words, alcohol disorders might both contribute to and result from adolescents' behavioral and affective problems.

Other findings from Clark and Bukstein's study include:

- Teens with psychological disorders tend to go rapidly from taking a first drink to becoming dependent on alcohol.

- Teens who abuse or are dependent on alcohol tend to have histories of childhood physical and sexual abuse; the girls are likely to have major depression or even post-traumatic stress disorder.

- Comprehensive treatment approaches that target coexisting alcohol and psychological disorders hold the most promise.

Out of Harm's Way

Can adolescents' alcohol use be predicted, and thereby prevented? Michael Windle of the University of Alabama at Birmingham explores three theories that attempt to answer this question. One theory suggests that some adolescents possess certain temperamental characteristics (such as high activity levels and abnormal behaviors) that predispose them toward early alcohol use.

A second theory attributes adolescent alcohol use to negative family and peer influences. Early onset drinking is a risk for kids from families that provide low levels of nurturing and supervision, inconsistent rules and expectations, and a tolerant or permissive attitude toward alcohol use. In line with this theory, researchers find that having siblings and friends who drink is a strong predictor of adolescent alcohol use.

A third theory proposes that many adolescents (like many adults) drink to avoid stress and to escape or avoid unpleasant moods. Kids who believe that drinking alcohol relieves stress are highly susceptible to drinking and developing alcohol-related problems.

A recent study of children's images of alcohol further explains this theory. Mark Goldman of the University of South Florida reports that, in early childhood, most children perceive alcohol negatively—usually as a drink that makes grown-ups sick, mean, and argumentative. But by fifth and sixth grade, many preteens begin to view alcohol as a drink that makes people happy, sociable, and appealing. Youngsters with strong, positive perceptions about alcohol are more likely to begin drinking early in adolescence, Goldman reports.

Predicting adolescent alcohol abuse is an inexact science, but new research studies show what works in preventing early drinking—and what doesn't work. As Windle points out, many intervention programs aimed at reducing or eliminating adolescent alcohol use focus on a single factor, such as peer pressure, instead of the complex array of factors that contribute to early drinking. These programs might be easier to manage, he says, but they're likely to have limited success.

A one-size-fits-all approach also leads to problems. School-based and community-based intervention programs should take into account students' risk factors at various ages and stages of development, Windle says. Intervention programs for early adolescents, for instance, are more successful when they target family involvement, but interventions for middle adolescents and older teens work best by emphasizing peer relationships.

Promising Results

A national intervention program that heeds these warnings is CASASTART (Striving Together to Achieve Rewarding Tomorrows), developed by the National Center on Addiction and Substance Abuse (CASA) at Columbia University. The program targets 8- to 13-year-olds, but it also involves parents, school staff, law enforcement personnel, and social service and health providers.

Students are eligible for the program's interventions if they show at least four risk factors in the following broad categories:

- *School risk*: low academic performance, behavior problems, and truancy

- *Family risk*: family violence, criminal involvement, substance use and sales, and extreme poverty

- *Personal risk*: substance use or sales, arrest or involvement in delinquent acts, gang membership, serious emotional disturbance, weapons possession, pregnancy or parenthood, suffering from abuse or maltreatment, or living in a dangerous neighborhood.

Case managers work with groups of 15 high-risk students to help keep them from taking their first drink or trying their first drug. Interventions include:

- Helping kids develop positive relationships with significant adults

- Organizing time for kids to interact positively with peers in free-time activities

- Creating opportunities for kids to form strong school attachments

- Countering negative influences from high-risk peers

- Improving communication between parents and kids

- Encouraging school attendance, good behavior, and academic achievement

- Helping parents and school personnel work together in positive ways

- Working with community members to reduce drug and alcohol sales

- Facilitating better relationships among police, youth, and families.

Program evaluations conducted in six cities show promising results. The Urban Institute, in collaboration with CASA and the National Institute of Justice, determined that children in the program, compared with those in matched control groups, had less substance use, fewer violent offenses, less association with delinquent peers, and less negative peer influence. Equally hopeful, CASASTART kids were more likely to succeed in school and be promoted to the next grade.

The boys who drank their days away in middle school, and the little girl who became a down-and-out alcoholic in sixth grade, aren't just statistics. They're real kids whose first drink took away their childhood and, perhaps, their future. Remembering these youngsters, and rescuing others from a similar fate, should be at the heart of school and community programs intent on keeping kids alcohol-free.

CONTEMPORARY
ISSUES
COMPANION

CHAPTER 3

Underage Drinking and the Media

Underage Drinking Is a Public Health Crisis

Joseph A. Califano Jr.

Joseph A. Califano Jr. is the chairman and president of the National Center on Addiction and Substance Abuse at Columbia University (CASA), an organization committed to studying and combating substance abuse in all sectors of society. Asserting that the United States is in the midst of an underage-drinking epidemic, Califano comments on the role that the alcohol industry plays in enticing millions of teens to drink its products. The author observes that this industry has been reprehensible in its promotion of television advertising campaigns that appeal to underage drinkers. Further, Califano derides alcohol lobbyists who persuaded the U.S. Congress not to grant the White House Office of National Drug Control Policy the authority to include alcohol in its drug prevention media campaign, even though alcohol is the drug most frequently abused by American teens.

Alcohol is far and away the top drug of abuse by America's teens. Children under the age of 21 drink 19.7 percent of the alcohol consumed in the U.S. More than five million high school students (31.5 percent) admit to binge drinking at least once a month. The age at which children begin drinking is dropping: since 1975, the proportion of children who begin drinking in the eighth grade or earlier has jumped by almost a third, from 27 to 36 percent. And the gender gap that for generations separated alcohol consumption by girls and boys has evaporated: male and female ninth graders are just as likely to drink (40.2 percent and 41 percent) and binge drink (21.7 percent and 20.2 percent).

Joseph A. Califano Jr., "Statement on the release of Teen Tipplers: America's Underage Drinking Epidemic," The National Center on Addiction and Substance Abuse at Columbia University. Reproduced by permission.

By any public health standard, America has an epidemic of underage drinking that germinates in elementary and middle schools with children nine to 13-years old and erupts on college campuses where 44 percent of students binge drink and alcohol is the number one substance of abuse—implicated in date rape, sexual harassment, racial disturbances, drop outs, overdose deaths from alcohol poisoning and suicides. Teenagers who drink are seven times likelier to engage in sex and twice as likely to have sex with four or more partners than those who do not. Such behavior can lead to unprotected sex with the increased risk of AIDS, other sexually transmitted diseases and pregnancy. Preliminary studies have shown that alcohol damages young minds, limiting mental and social development. High schoolers who drink are five times likelier to drop out of school.

No other substance threatens as many of the nation's children. Eighty percent of high school students have tried alcohol, while 70 percent have smoked cigarettes and 47 percent have used marijuana. Twenty-nine percent of high school seniors have used some other illegal drug such as Ecstasy.

Drinking is teen America's fatal attraction. Beer and other alcohol are implicated in the three top causes of teen deaths: accidents (including traffic fatalities and drowning), homicide and suicide. The financial costs of underage drinking approach $53 billion in accidents, drowning, burns, violent crime, suicide attempts, fetal alcohol syndrome, alcohol poisoning and emergency medical care. Teens who experiment with alcohol are virtually certain to continue using it. Among high school seniors who have ever tried alcohol—even once— 91.3 percent are still drinking in twelfth grade. Most troubling, of high school students who have ever been drunk, 83.3 percent—more than two million teens—are still getting drunk in twelfth grade.

This report makes clear: the time and place to deal with binge drinking in college is in elementary and high school.

Teen drinking is the number one source of adult alcoholism. Children who begin drinking before age 21 are more than twice as likely to develop alcohol-related problems. Those who begin drinking before age 15 are four times likelier to become alcoholics than those who do not drink before age 21.

Underage drinkers are at greater risk of nicotine and illegal drug addiction. Teens who are heavy drinkers (consume at least five drinks on at least five occasions over 30 days) are more than 12 times likelier to use illegal drugs than those who do not drink.

How did we get here?

We have to point the finger at ourselves.

Parents tend to see drinking and occasional bingeing as a rite of passage, rather than a deadly round of Russian roulette. Home—a child's or a child's friend's—is a major source of alcohol for children, especially for younger children. A third of sixth and ninth graders obtain alcohol from their own homes. Children cite other people's houses as the most common setting for drinking. In our schools, middle and high school teachers have been reluctant to inform parents or intervene when they suspect a child or teen of drinking. College administrators and alumni have played Pontius Pilate, washing their hands and looking away, as students made beer, alcohol and binge drinking a central part of their college experience. The pervasive influence of the entertainment media has glamorized and sexualized alcohol and rarely shown the ill effects of abuse. A review of 81 G-rated animated films found that in 34 percent of them alcohol use was associated with wealth or luxury and 19 percent associated alcohol with sexual activity.

Television runs ads glorifying beer on sports programs watched by millions of children and teens. With a big push from alcohol lobbyists, the Congress has denied the White House Office of National Drug Control Policy authority to include alcohol—the number one drug of abuse by children and teens—in its media campaign and other activities to prevent drug abuse.

The interest of the alcohol industry—especially those who sell beer—in underage drinking is understandable, if appalling. Underage drinkers are a critical segment of the alcohol beverage market. Underage drinkers consume 19.7 percent of the alcohol—most often beer—sold in this country. In 1999, they accounted for approximately $22.5 billion of the $116.2 billion spent on alcohol, including as much as $17.2 billion on beer. Without underage drinkers, the alcohol industry, and the beer industry in particular, would suffer severe economic declines and dramatic loss of profits.

Drawn from CASA's [The National Center on Addiction and Substance Abuse at Columbia University] innovative National Underage Drinking Survey of adults, this report calls for a national mobilization to curb underage drinking. It sets out actions for parents, law enforcement, legislators, the entertainment industry and for a measure of self control by the beer, wine and liquor industries. It will take all of that to save millions of teens from destroying their lives through alcohol abuse. Our children are our future and, for adults, the future is now in mounting a national effort to curb teen drinking. This survey provides a road map of citizens' attitudes to guide federal, state and local officials interested in promoting public policies to reduce teen use of alcohol and binge drinking.

The prevention message is more difficult to convey with regard to alcohol. For smoking and illegal drug use, the message is, "No!" for children and adults. For alcohol, the message is "No!" for children under 21 (except for certain family and cultural occasions), but for most adults (those who are not alcoholics or alcohol abusers) the message is moderation, not prohibition.

The NCAA Should Ban Beer Advertisements at Its Sporting Events

Amy E. Gotwals, Jay Hedlund, and George A. Hacker

The Center for Science in the Public Interest (CSPI) is a non-profit health-advocacy organization that manages research and educational programs centering on nutrition, food safety, and alcohol policy. In the following article, Amy Gotwals, Jay Hedlund, and George A. Hacker maintain that the National Collegiate Athletic Association (NCAA) engages in a conflict of interest by marketing its athletic programs, including the popular NCAA basketball tournament, to children and teenagers while it also accepts advertising revenue from alcohol producers who run commercials at NCAA sporting events. The authors contend that the alcohol industry should not be marketing its products to an NCAA audience that is comprised of significant numbers of children and teens. They also suggest that the NCAA undermines the educational mission of its constituent colleges and universities because alcohol ads from NCAA sporting events encourage viewers to begin drinking at an early age, a circumstance that often leads to college binge drinking, low academic achievement, and a decreased wage-earning potential.

The NCAA [National Collegiate Athletic Association] expends considerable effort promoting its worthy "attributes" to children and teenagers as it recruits them as current and future fans and consumers. The NCAA brand conjures a youth-friendly, wholesome, and healthy image with high-minded, important ideals. Those ideals provide an ap-

Amy E. Gotwals, Jay Hedlund, and George A. Hacker, *Take a Kid to a Beer: How the NCAA Recruits Kids for the Beer Market.* Danvers, MA: Center for Science in the Public Interest, 2005. Copyright © 2005 by Center for Science in the Public Interest. Republished with permission of Center for Science in the Public Interest, conveyed through Copyright Clearance Center, Inc.

pealing image for product marketers who invest substantially to reach the important youth demographic delivered by the NCAA.

Beer makers, who ranked third among advertisers on televised sports—ahead of fast-food, credit cards, computers, non-alcoholic beverages, financial services, and movies—are among those marketers that have the strongest designs on that target audience. And, whether a direct result of its youth-recruitment efforts or not, the NCAA delivers millions of children and teenagers (along with adults) to beer producers who hawk drinking to them during the NCAA's basketball championship tournament.

Intentional or not, the NCAA's dedicated youth-recruitment activities help provide a pipeline of impressionable underage people directly to beer marketers, adding to the goldmine of current consumers and the coveted young-adult target audience.

Brewers spend liberally to reach the college sports audience. In 2003, beer producers invested $52.2 million advertising on televised college sports. Bud Light led the way (with $11.4 million), followed by Miller Lite, Budweiser, and Coors Light.

The 2003 NCAA basketball tournament alone concentrated $21.1 million in beer ads into the three weeks of games watched by more than 6 million children and teens. In both 2001 and 2002, more beer ads ran on the NCAA broadcasts than during the World Series, all college football bowl games, the Super Bowl, and NFL Monday Night Football combined.

Notwithstanding the beer industry's ritual denials that its advertising targets underage consumers, its spokespeople routinely acknowledge the need to attract young consumers' attention. Anheuser-Busch's Tony Ponturo admits that the company strives for youthful edginess in its advertising, as leaning too old can make the product seem "stale." Not surprisingly, beer ads are among the most popular and memorable ads on television, both among adults and children.

Big Beer Needs New Drinkers

The beer industry has a strong economic interest in associating itself with the NCAA and its sports audience. Just as the NCAA constantly courts new young fans, so do brewers. They rely on young drinkers to replace customers who quit, cut down on their drinking as they age, or die. Brand identification occurs early in life, and, by the age of 21, many drinkers have already settled on a favorite. Brewers need to attract customers long before they reach the legal drinking age because, on average, drinkers begin consuming at age 16.

Brewers have more at stake than building brand awareness that may translate into future sales. Young people drink beer, and lots of it. In the 1990s, 18–34-year-olds, who "made up only about 20 [percent] of the total beer drinking population, consumed an estimated 70 [percent] of all beer in this country." And underage drinkers down much of it. Both binge and heavy drinking peak at age 21. More than a quarter (29.2 percent) of high school seniors report downing five or more drinks in a row in the past two weeks.

Although it is hard to establish the exact percentage of all beer consumed by underage persons, that amount must be substantial. Evidence reported in the *Journal of the American Medical Association* suggests that as much as 20 percent of all *alcohol* sold in the U.S. is consumed by persons under age 21, so it is not unreasonable to conclude that underage drinkers down a similar proportion of beer. After all, beer is the beverage of choice among younger drinkers. If one were to assume that underage drinkers consume just 15 percent of the beer sold in the U.S., that would account for some $12 billion in yearly beer sales, a fat chunk of industry revenue. By any definition, illicit consumption by consumers under age 21 constitutes an important, if not essential, part of the beer market.

Heavy drinkers (including many who are underage) comprise the other key market that drives beer sales. Ten percent of beer drinkers consume 43 percent of the beer in this country; 59 percent of beer is consumed in hazardous amounts in the U.S. Heavy drinkers *are* the beer market. And many of those beer guzzlers started early. The National Institute on Alcohol Abuse and Alcoholism reports that young people who start drinking by age 15 are four times as likely to become heavy, dependent drinkers than those who wait until they're 21. The beer industry certainly has a strong profit motive to appeal to consumers younger than 21.

Ads Affect Kids

Millions of youngsters watch NCAA basketball, which delivers them to advertisers for numerous products, including beer. Our conservative estimates indicate that more than six million fans under the age of 21 watched the 2005 NCAA men's basketball championship broadcast. Eugene Sacunda, an adjunct professor of media studies at New York University, who handled beer accounts as a vice president at the J. Walter Thompson ad agency, told National Public Radio that the beer ads he saw on the NCAA broadcast were, in part, aimed at preparing the younger, pre-drinking age audience to develop a positive brand awareness and a brand relationship with the beers advertised during the game.

Recent evidence suggests that youth exposure to beer ads on television has a measurable impact on underage drinking. Researchers have determined that "exposure to alcohol advertising increases the risk of subsequent alcohol use" among adolescents. Children who are exposed to more alcohol advertising "believe that drinking is more likely to have positive consequences, perceive higher levels of alcohol use by and approval of drinking by peers, have greater intentions to drink in the future, and have high levels of alcohol consumption." Exposure to beer advertisements significantly predicts adolescents' knowledge of beer brands, preference for beer brands, current drinking behaviors, beer-brand loyalty, and intentions to drink.

Although it may be difficult to establish a clear, causal connection between beer advertising and underage drinking, there can be no doubt that the ads glamorize drinking, suggest that drinking leads to good times and good friends, and thoroughly obscure the many risks related to alcohol consumption. Industry and NCAA claims that the ads' messages have no effect on underage drinking belie recent evidence and common sense. No one seems to question that similar ads for cigarettes attract young people to smoking.

Beer and Colleges Do Not Mix

Based on the beer industry's keen interest in marketing within the world of sports and its need to attract young consumers, it's not much of a surprise that the NCAA would be a natural venue for beer advertising. What is surprising, however, is the NCAA's acquiescence and participation in hawking beer to students and the many other young people who tune into the games.

Unlike beer marketers, who depend on it, the NCAA and its member schools don't benefit from beer consumption by students and other young fans. Beer and other alcohol consumption among college students too often translate into a steady source of problems. This context reveals the utter lack of principle in the NCAA's choice to promote beer consumption to young viewers.

Each year, 1,700 college students die and 500,000 are injured from related causes; 70,000 are sexually assaulted in alcohol-fueled attack. In 2002 alone, more than 10 alcohol-induced celebratory riots and campus disturbances erupted among sports fans at colleges across America. In 2001, two out of five college students were classified as binge drinkers. Almost half of all alcohol use reported by college students is attributable to those who are underage. And students who identify as sports fans are more likely to engage in binge drinking behavior, as well.

Those problems hit the core of universities' missions as well: high alcohol consumption is associated with lower grade point averages among students, lower academic achievement, and lower wage potential.

Many schools pay a steep price in campus property damage, lost tuition from drop outs and failures, personnel who have to deal with alcohol-related issues, college counseling centers, security staff, administrative hearings on academic and disciplinary cases, and the costs of litigation arising from alcohol-related harm. Intangible costs may include strains in the relationship between schools and surrounding communities, a diminished reputation, and the time lost and stress felt by college, staff members who work on alcohol-related issues.

Alcohol Appeals to Teens

College students are not alone among youth in abusing alcohol: alcohol is the drug of choice among American youth. One in five 15-year-olds reported drinking in the past month. Thirty-seven percent of sixth, seventh, and eighth graders reported drinking alcohol in 2002–2003, many of them at dangerously high levels. More than half (60.3 percent) of high school seniors have been drunk, and more than a quarter (29.2 percent) report downing five or more drinks in a row in the past two weeks. Alcohol is a significant factor in the four leading causes of death among persons aged 10 to 24: motor-vehicle crashes, unintentional injuries, homicide, and suicide.

With that backdrop, the NCAA's advertising policy, which proclaims that ads should be in the "best interests of higher education," reveals more than a touch of irony. Pitching beer to students and other young fans during NCAA games counters the educational mission of the NCAA and its member colleges and undercuts the many costly prevention measures taken on those campuses today.

Few college presidents fail to acknowledge the fundamental disconnect between a university's commitment to reducing harms from binge and underage drinking and allowing alcohol ads on college sports broadcasts. Beer marketers want to sell beer—as much of it as possible; the NCAA's mission focuses on developing and nurturing student-athletes and athletics in higher education. The two are simply incompatible. As former Ohio State University athletic director Andy Geiger asserts: "It's inconsistent to say you want to discourage underage drinking and turn around and huckster the stuff on your broadcast."

Alcohol Industry Is Committed to Reducing Underage Drinking

National Research Council Institute of Medicine

As part of its comprehensive investigation of the problem of underage alcohol abuse, the Committee on Developing a Strategy to Reduce and Prevent Underage Drinking evaluates the voluntary prevention strategies that the alcohol industry has employed in an effort to keep its products out of the hands of children. The committee surveys a number of industry-sponsored prevention initiatives, including "We I.D.," a law enforcement program that requires retailers to ask patrons for personal identification before they can purchase alcohol. The committee also acknowledges the concerns of alcohol industry critics who argue that many of the industry's early prevention programs are cleverly designed to promote brand identification with youths who will potentially become consumers of alcohol products when they reach the legal drinking age. Due to the perceived equivocal nature of the alcohol industry's commitment to preventing underage drinking, the committee recommends that all segments of the industry should charter and fund an independent nonprofit foundation whose exclusive mission is to reduce and prevent drinking by minors.

The alcoholic beverage industry—the brewers, vintners, and producers of distilled spirits—and the distributors and servers of these products—have been an important part of U.S. society from its colonial beginnings. Indeed, it was in the "public houses" where "potables" were served that much of the planning for the American Revolution was accomplished. Part of that tradition, however, has been a general under-

National Research Council Institute of Medicine, *Reducing Underage Drinking: A Collective Responsibility*. Washington, DC: The National Academics Press, 2004. Copyright © 2004 by the National Academy of Sciences, courtesy of the National Academies Press, Washington, D.C. All rights reserved. Reproduced by permission.

standing that while alcohol is woven into the fabric of the nation's collective life, it also has great potential for causing harm, and that producers, distributors, and servers of alcohol bear some of the responsibility for preventing that harm and for promoting safe and responsible drinking. That is at least part of what it meant to be a "publican"—a position of significant status and responsibility in colonial society. That idea survives today in the licensing requirements for drinking establishments, in the existence of a structure of server liability, and in the commitment of the alcohol producers to encourage responsible drinking.

It is clear, we think, that those who produce and distribute alcohol have the opportunity to act in ways that will either ameliorate or exacerbate the problem of underage drinking. We take at face value the industry's collective commitment to helping society manage and reduce underage drinking. Such a declaration of values and intentions is consistent with a common-sense understanding of the industry's social and legal responsibility with respect to underage drinking. Yet two important social realities are inescapable: first, that a significant amount of underage drinking occurs in violation of the law and against the stated intentions of the industry, and second, that the alcohol beverage industry gains financial returns (both revenues and profits) from underage drinking.

Some Question Industry's Commitment to Preventing Underage Drinking

Some have taken these facts to suggest that the alcohol industry's commitment to reducing underage drinking may be equivocal. After all, today's underage drinkers are tomorrow's legitimate customers, and the industry has self-evident economic incentives to satisfy the underage demand. Suspicion that some new alcohol products and some alcohol advertising seem to be specifically targeted at the tastes and sensibilities of underage drinkers leads some industry critics to claim that at least some companies are not only being negligent with respect to underage drinking, but may (more culpably) be encouraging it.

In this report we take the industry's professed motives as its true motives and focus our attention on how the industry's collective efforts to reduce underage drinking could become both more effective and more credible. In the committee's judgment, a great deal can and should be done by the alcohol industry to help society prevent and ameliorate some of the harms associated with its otherwise legitimate efforts to produce and market a product valued by the adult population. Specifically, the industry's commendable investment in programs to reduce underage drinking or promote responsible adult drinking warrant more rigorous evaluation and improved coordination with other efforts. The committee makes several recommendations designed to increase and channel the industry's prevention efforts.

Industry Programs to Reduce and Prevent Underage Drinking

In recognition of the high prevalence of underage and illegal drinking, the alcohol industry has declared its collective support of the 21-year-old minimum drinking age and has undertaken efforts to discourage alcohol use by underage youths. Various industry-sponsored initiatives and programs have been implemented with the stated objectives of reducing underage drinking and promoting responsible or moderate drinking among adults. The Beer Institute, the national trade association for the nation's brewers, reported that the beer industry has "committed hundreds of millions of dollars to create effective anti-underage drinking programs." For example, Anheuser-Busch and its wholesalers have "invested more than $375 million [time period not specified] to implement alcohol awareness programs to fight drunk driving, help retailers spot fake IDs, and encourage parents to talk with their kids about drinking."

Beer producers and wholesalers have produced numerous brochures, booklets, compact disks, videos, and public service announcements aimed at educating youth, parents, potential servers of alcohol to youth, and the general public. Programs for servers of alcohol (e.g., "We I.D.," "TIPS") are designed to promote enforcement of laws prohibiting sales to minors and to prevent serving underage and intoxicated persons. Other materials highlight the perils of drinking and driving, promote responsible drinking, or provide advice to parents on helping kids make responsible decisions. The industry also has sponsored activities specific to college campuses. They include the types of activities just noted, as well as support for the social norms approach (i.e., counteracting beliefs that the prevalence of drinking among peers is higher than it really is). Some companies in the beer industry also have sponsored public speakers and participated in community efforts to address underage drinking.

Representatives of the distilled spirits industry reported to the committee a similar commitment to reducing underage drinking. For example, the Distilled Spirits Council of the United States (DISCUS), a national trade association representing producers and marketers of distilled sprits and importers of wines sold in the United States, recently provided funding to a number of colleges to implement alcohol action plans. DISCUS also supports the programs funded by the Century Council, a nonprofit entity established in 1991 that reports having invested "more than $120 million" over the last 10 years "in programs that fight against the misuse of their products." The Century Council defines its core activities as being aimed at four objectives, two of which focus on drunk driving and two of which focus specifically on underage drinking:

- educate middle-school through college students, their parents, teachers, and adult caregivers about the importance of making responsible decisions regarding beverage alcohol;

- inform the public about how gender, weight, and number and type of drink affect an individual's blood alcohol concentration (BAC) and increase awareness of state BAC driving laws;

- deter minors from buying beverage alcohol through joint programs with law enforcement, retailers, and wholesalers, using point-of-sale materials and public awareness campaigns; and

- reduce drunk driving through research and promising strategies, tougher state and federal legislation, treatment, and education.

In addition to activities similar to those described above, the Century Council has produced resource materials (e.g., *Promising Practices: Campus Alcohol Strategies*) aimed at helping colleges develop effective programs to reduce alcohol abuse. They also have developed and distributed Alcohol 101, a college-level interactive program on alcohol-related problems that is distributed to hundreds of campuses nationwide and Cops in Shops, a program aimed at deterring underage purchases.

Overall, the alcohol industry has apparently invested significant resources in a diverse range of efforts aimed at reducing underage drinking and its associated harms, including media messages, educational programs, and enforcement activities. Some industry members have also entered into partnerships with specific colleges and universities to reduce drinking problems on those campuses, often grounded in social norms marketing approaches.

Evaluating Alcohol 101

The committee is aware of only one industry-sponsored education program that has been independently evaluated—Alcohol 101. The evaluation used a naturalistic design with purposeful sampling, including attention to regional sampling, and included colleges and universities believed to have done a good job implementing the program. [The independent evaluators] Anderson and Cohen reported that the program is viewed "with a high degree of positive regard," with some campus personnel suggesting modest changes on their campuses, and others reporting positive student engagement. Anderson and Cohen reported, with the most robust implementations, measurable gains in relevant knowledge, willingness to act in emergencies, and intentions to modify drinking to reduce alcohol problems. Nonetheless, they suggested additional in-depth analysis of the campus-based findings involving additional institutions and types of settings and further statistical analyses of existing data.

A recent study by the Center on Alcohol Marketing and Youth (2003) studied "responsibility advertising" by the alcohol industry on television in 2001 and reported that industry spent $23.2 million to air 2,379 responsibility messages (discouraging underage drinking and drunk driving); they contrasted these with $811.2 on 208,909 product advertisements. With regard to underage drinking in particular, they report that there were 179 product ads for every ad that referred to the legal drinking age. All of the legal-drinking age messages were broadcast by only two alcohol companies—Anheuser Busch ($12.2 million) and Coors ($3.6 million).

Do Underage Drinking Programs Promote Brand Identification?

Many public health experts in the alcohol prevention field are highly skeptical about the value of the industry's underage drinking programs and other prevention activities and about the industry's collective motivation for sponsoring them. The criticism most frequently heard is that the main effect of these programs may be to promote brand identification, if not alcohol use itself. The committee is in no position to assess or ascertain the actual intentions underlying these programs. However, in the absence of documented evidence of effectiveness from independent evaluation, skepticism about the value of industry-sponsored programs is likely to continue. Based on our own review of the materials submitted by industry representatives, the alcohol prevention literature, and the other materials and testimony submitted to the committee, we believe that industry efforts to prevent and reduce underage drinking, however sincere, should be redirected and strengthened.

Industry Should Fund Independent Foundation

Other public health leaders have recently urged the alcohol industry to endow an independent foundation to curb excessive drinking by adults as well as underage drinking. However, the committee believes that—at the outset, at least—the mission should be strictly limited to the prevention of underage drinking. If the mission is not limited to underage drinking, which is illegal, the committee is doubtful that agreement could be reached about the foundation's goals and the scope of its activities. While a very strong social consensus supports strong measures to reduce underage drinking, such a consensus does not yet exist about what it means to reduce "excessive" or otherwise "irresponsible" drinking or about the measures that should be taken to achieve this goal.

The committee believes that a foundation that is focused exclusively on preventing and reducing underage drinking— through activities, programs, and methods that can be carefully defined and specified in the founding charter—would provide an opportunity for the alcohol industry, interested business associations, advocacy organizations, and government to enter into a social contract grounded in, and manifesting, recognition of collective responsibility. Primary funding for such a foundation would ideally be provided by alcohol producers and wholesalers as an offset to income they receive as a result of underage drinking. By contributing to the foundation, they would have an opportunity to acknowledge, without defensiveness, that marketing of alcohol to young adults contributes, however unintentionally, to the web of social influences promoting underage drinking. The foundation also would provide an opportunity for all member organizations to declare and implement a genuine and unequivocal commitment to try to curtail alcohol use by underage youths and to conduct impartial evaluation of the effectiveness of interventions undertaken.

As the committee envisions it, many, if not all, of the existing industry activities in the domain of underage drinking would be redirected to the new foundation. The committee is in no position to write the charter for this entity, which will have to be negotiated among all the organizational participants. However, it is clear that the charter would have to ensure that the foundation's ability to operate is not hampered by the dominance of any single interest group or by the perception that it serves the commercial interests of its funders. A possible funding formula among all the participating industry partners could be developed along the following lines: Each alcohol producer, acting individually or through trade associations or other entities, would help to fund the activities of the foundation in a manner that is commensurate with the amount and proportion of industry revenues attributable to underage consumption. . . . Underage drinkers consumed between 10 and 20 percent of all alcohol consumed in 2000, representing about $11 to 22 billion, although the proportion differs substantially among beer, wine, and spirits. A reasonable target for the annual industry contribution to the foundation would be 0.5 percent of gross revenues (about $250–500 million) prorated according to the particular company's share of the underage market (estimated based on surveys about underage brand use, or, in the absence of such data, based on the particular company's share of the overall beer, wine, or spirits market).

Interim Measures to Prevent Underage Drinking Urged

Until the proposed foundation has been established, the committee believes that the alcohol industry should take two immediate steps to redirect the resources and activities currently devoted to preventing underage drinking and to move toward the strategy recommended by the committee. First, industry-sponsored media messages regarding underage drinking should be redirected away from youth audiences and focused instead on changing the attitudes and behavior of parents and other adults—to persuade them not to facilitate or enable underage drinking and to accept responsibility for preventing it. For example, industry-sponsored messages could be designed to alert adults to their legal responsibilities, including potential liability for injuries caused by underage drinkers to whom they give alcohol, or could show a shoulder-tap enforcement sting by undercover youths. Although the alcohol industry may not be the most credible source of messages aiming to reduce the demand for alcohol (by either adults or youths), messages aimed specifically at curbing behaviors that violate the restrictions on underage access can hardly be used as pretexts to stimulate demand. Indeed, they might be especially effective because the industry has both credibility and natural channels of communication with its adult customers. Second, industry-funded messages and programs should be delivered directly to young people only if they rest on a scientific foundation, as judged by qualified, independent organizations, or incorporate rigorous evaluation. Programs that have an exclusive focus on providing information have been demonstrated to be ineffective at reducing alcohol use and should be avoided.

CHAPTER 4

Personal Narratives on Teenage Alcohol Abuse

Binge Drinking Can Be Fatal

Anne Mullens

In the following article, Anne Mullens provides a collection of anecdotes about teens and young adults who have abused alcohol by engaging in binge drinking. The author points out that while illicit drug use in general is on the decline among fifteen- to twenty-five-year-old users, alcohol abuse in this age group has remained steady and in some cases has increased. Mullens also details the potentially hazardous health consequences for teens who drink heavily, focusing on long-term brain damage and death by alcohol poisoning.

Julian remembers little of his lost Friday night in October 2003 except that he was drinking vodka shooters in a friend's room at McGill University and having a great time. "I must have drunk most of a full 26er [twenty-six ounces of alcohol]," recalls the 20-year-old political-science student. At around 10 p.m., his friends say, they all walked out across the campus, searching for another party, but Julian somehow wandered off. He woke up hours later, lying in a bed in the emergency room of the Montreal General Hospital, smelling of vomit and alcohol. "To this day, I have no idea how I got there," he says sheepishly.

Jeff recalls drinking "way too many" beers, tequila shots and whisky and stumbling out of a friend's party in Dundas, Ont., last year at age 17, vomiting in the bushes and then crawling into the back seat of a car. He awoke to the glaring probe of a flashlight from a police officer who called his dismayed parents to take the inebriated teen home.

Evan, a 17-year-old student in West Vancouver [British Columbia], was the designated driver at a friend's party one

Anne Mullens, "The Perils of Binge Drinking," *Reader's Digest* (Canada), September 2005. Reprinted by permission from the September 2005 *Reader's Digest*.

night when someone shoved an incoherent, drunken Grade 9 girl into his car with the request to "take her home." With no idea who she was or where she belonged, and worried that she may be close to alcohol poisoning, he and a friend put the semiconscious girl in a wheelchair inside the doors of the Lion's Gate Hospital in North Vancouver and drove away. "She was so drunk we thought she might die, but we didn't stay because we thought we'd get in trouble," says Evan, who later learned the girl spent the night in hospital, sobering up under the watchful eyes of emergency staff.

These stories all feature good kids who were involved in binge drinking. They were lucky; none died or drove drunk or had any of the many calamities that can arise from a night of heavy drinking.

Health and Social Consequences

Most Canadians appreciate a cold beer on a hot day or a glass of wine at dinner. That kind of responsible use of alcohol is a social lubricant that makes life a little more pleasant.

But binge drinking is different. Call it getting tanked, sloshed, blotto—binge drinking is typically defined as consuming five or more drinks for a man and four or more drinks for a woman on a single occasion. That's enough to impair judgement, impede coordination, remove inhibitions, cause slurring of words—and potentially put someone at risk of serious health or social consequences, lasting brain damage and even death.

Binge drinking, of course, is not confined to teenagers or young adults. Nor is it new. People have been getting drunk since early humans fermented the first home brew. But what alarms public-health officials is the fact that while illicit drug use has generally been declining, the prevalence of binge drinking has been holding steady and even increasing, particularly among youth age 15 to 25. Moreover, new studies show that some kids start drinking at 13 or younger, and youth are particularly at risk from its effects.

"It is a huge issue," says Dr. Stephen Wheeler, chief of emergency medicine for the Vancouver Island Health Authority, who notes that each Friday or Saturday night it is common to have at least four or five binge drinkers—many under 25—brought in for injuries or for monitoring in Victoria's two hospital emergency departments.

Adolescent Binge Drinking on the Rise

Recent surveys of binge drinking patterns among youth are "sobering":

- In Ontario, 83 percent of Grade 12 students drink, and 45 percent have had at least one episode of binge drinking in the previous four weeks, according to the 2003 Ontario Student Drug Use Survey. While the percentage of students binge drinking increases with each grade, the biggest single increase—from eight to 24 percent—occurs between Grades 8 and 9. "That jump tells us that a significant number of kids are starting really young," says Edward Adlaf, coauthor of the study.

- A 2003 survey of British Columbia high-school students conducted by the McCreary Centre Society found that 46 percent of males and 43 percent of females in high school who admitted to drinking had engaged in binge drinking in the previous month, a rate that is among the highest in Canada and unchanged since 1998.

- Binge drinking is particularly worrisome on university and college campuses in Canada and the United States. Four surveys of 120 U.S. campuses over the last decade found that 44 percent of students admitted to an episode of binge drinking in the two weeks prior to the survey, a rate that has remained unchanged for a decade. The 2000 Canadian Campus Survey found similar results, with 63 percent of students reporting consuming five or more drinks in a single sitting in the previous year. The Canadian study concluded that campuses are a "risky milieu for hazardous drinking."

Julian at McGill agrees. "It doesn't matter where you go in Canada. On most campuses there's a focus on 'partying'—which means getting drunk."

A Public Health Problem

The words "alcohol abuse" and "problem drinker" typically conjure up the image of a chronic alcoholic, but in fact fewer than five percent of Canadians are alcohol dependent. Of college students, says Henry Wechsler of Harvard's School of Public Health, only about six percent fit the definition of "alcoholic." But binge drinking is more of a public-health problem than alcoholism as it affects a higher percentage of young drinkers.

"The probability of developing liver cirrhosis or cancer is based on the amount of tissue exposure to alcohol over many years, but every time people binge drink, they place themselves at increased risk of harming themselves or others—even if it is the very first time a person drinks," says Jurgen Rehm, a leading expert on problem drinking.

Whatever the age, binge drinking puts a person at much higher risk of death or injuries from motor vehicle crashes, falls, drowning and other hazards of poor judgement and reduced coordination. Violence, vandalism, sexual assault, unprotected sexual encounters with the risk of unplanned pregnancy or infection from sexually transmitted diseases all increase.

Alcohol Abuse Can Lead to Brain Damage

New research also shows that young people, whose brains are still developing, may be at greater risk than mature adults of lasting brain damage from heavy alcohol consumption.

"We are seeing significant differences in abilities in the brains of young people who drink heavily on a regular basis," says Susan Tapert, associate professor of psychiatry at the University of California [San Diego] and one of the leading researchers using magnetic resonance imaging to assess the impact of binge drinking on the brain in youth. "Drinking to intoxication seems to be particularly associated with poorer functioning on tests of learning and memory and on visual-spatial tasks such as doing a puzzle," says Tapert, who notes that since teenagers mature at different rates, the brains of youth anywhere between age 13 and the early 20s may be at risk. "As a mother, I'm concerned about my children's potential to drink in adolescence and have lasting brain effects."

Alcohol Poisoning Can Be Fatal

Another tragic danger of binge drinking—one often wrapped in stigma and silence—is the risk of death from alcohol poisoning, also called alcohol overdose. Alcohol is a central-nervous-system depressant, and it is fatally toxic at high levels. When blood alcohol levels climb rapidly, the body's natural reflex is to vomit to purge itself of the poison.

Drinking too much too fast can shut down key bodily functions such as gag reflexes, breathing, heart rate and brain function. The result can be choking on vomit, coma or cardiac arrest.

Rehm notes that 68 Canadians died of alcohol poisoning in 2002, "but that is likely a significant under-reporting" in part because of the lingering stigma of drinking oneself to death. With no requirement to report alcohol poisonings, doctors or coroners may instead put "asphyxiation" or "cardiac arrest" as the cause of death.

Unaccustomed to alcohol, young people often rapidly consume excessive amounts that push their blood alcohol concentrations to dangerously high levels. Since it takes at least 30 minutes for alcohol to be fully absorbed by the small intestine and enter the blood stream, binge drinkers can ingest a fatal dose of alcohol before passing out.

Prevention Programs Aim to Educate Kids

The P.A.R.T.Y. (Prevent Alcohol and Risk-Related Trauma in Youth) program began at Toronto's Sunnybrook and Women's College Health Science Centre in 1986. "We wanted to show kids what can happen when you make bad choices, such as drinking too much," says Joanne Banfield, founder of the first P.A.R.T.Y. program. Now in 68 hospitals in Canada and the United States, the program gives tours to thousands of high-school students each year through hospital emergency departments, intensive-care units, rehabilitation units and . . . morgues.

Recently in Victoria, 75 Grade 10 students toured Victoria General Hospital and heard Dr. Wheeler and others—such as a local police officer, a paramedic, a coroner and a victim—describe in graphic detail their stories of youth-related trauma, often caused by binge drinking.

"This is what happens when your face goes through a windshield," said Wheeler, showing a photograph of a girl with extreme facial lacerations that elicited horrified gasps from the teens. Said one 15-year-old boy: "It was the most graphic presentation I've ever seen. It certainly makes you stop and think."

Parents Should Be Positive Role Models

Parents can do their part, too. Setting minimum prices for drinks in bars and raising the drinking age to 21, argues Rehm, are two actions provincial governments could take. Lowering the driving-impaired limit to .05 blood/alcohol concentration is being promoted by Mothers Against Drunk Drivers and other organizations as a way to further bring down the toll of drinking and driving.

Parents have a key role in reducing binge drinking, such as not serving alcohol to teenagers and by talking openly to their teens about the risks and by modelling responsible behaviour. "If you drink to excess regularly or drink and drive, there is little you can say to your teens that will make a difference," says Wechsler. "Show them how to drink responsibly—by drinking responsibly yourself."

Police Deal with Out-of-Control Teen Parties and Irresponsible Parents

Ruth Padawer and Leslie Brody

Ruth Padawer and Leslie Brody report on the experiences of New Jersey police officers who frequently disrupt house parties where teenage kids are caught drinking alcohol and doing drugs. The police officers recount stories about how they have discovered teenagers who become unconscious or choke on their own vomit from drinking too much, how kids have broken bones attempting to flee the scene of a party, and how drunken minors have mangled themselves in car accidents after attending a party. The police also relate to the authors their continuing disbelief at the irresponsibility of countless parents who allow their kids to go to parties where alcohol and drugs are present, who are oblivious to what their children are doing at these parties, or who actually supply the alcohol and allow kids to use their own house for a party. The authors conclude that while it is often hard for parents to communicate with their teenagers, the consequences for not addressing the problem of underage drinking with their kids can be tragic.

By the time police waded through the empty Budweiser cans and Jack Daniel's [whiskey] bottles, most of the kids had fled. Left behind was a floor awash in alcohol and cellphones that no teenager would ordinarily abandon.

North Haledon [New Jersey] police found teens hiding in attic closets, alongside the basement sump pump and throughout the nearby woods. And to the officers' amazement, the parents of the 15-year-old host had been home the whole time.

Ruth Padawer and Leslie Brody, "Dangerous Brew," NorthJersey.com, May 21, 2006. Reproduced by permission.

The scene—a potent brew of teenagers, alcohol and bewildered parents—is common every weekend throughout New Jersey. One in three New Jersey high school students consumes five drinks in a row at least once a month, one study found. Yet other surveys show that many parents underestimate their own children's indulgences, or intentionally look away. Some even supply the alcohol.

In Westwood, police rounded up 22 teens and charged one of their mothers with providing alcohol. In Alpine, police nabbed 30 kids and charged a 14-year-old boy with serving minors at a party he'd held while his parents were away. In Glen Rock, police charged four girls, including two 13-year-olds, with underage drinking after one swilled so much 90-proof banana rum that her friends had to drag her, semiconscious, out of the woods.

"We call them baby drunks," said Riverdale police Lt. John Peine.

Although most parents are petrified of losing their children to drunken driving, far fewer worry about the other social, emotional and health problems that underage drinking can cause. Young people who drink before age 15 are four times more likely to become alcoholics than those who start after 20. And because their still-developing brains respond more slowly to alcohol, kids drink a lot before feeling the effects. Studies show when the alcohol finally hits, it makes the impulsiveness of adolescence even more dangerous.

Emergency room doctors tell of drunken teenagers who have choked on vomit, cut tendons punching through windows, broken bones falling from fences and roofs, poisoned themselves into oblivion or wound up mangled in car crashes. They are images doctors take home.

"Watch out," John LoCurto, trauma director at Hackensack University Medical Center, frequently tells his 19-year-old son. "One moment of stupidity and you'll pay for it the rest of your life."

"We Have a Problem"

Word of the St. Paddy's Day party in North Haledon had bounced from cellphone to cellphone, computer to computer. By 8 p.m., the get-together was under way, as kids from all over Bergen and Passaic counties started showing up at the modest house nestled against the woods. The frolicking spilled into the street.

Shortly after 9, a neighbor called police, complaining that rowdy kids were running up and down the street, kicking over planters and yelling.

Police records, the police chief, and a detective and a sergeant who were on the scene and interviewed partygoers, provide an account of what happened that evening. Police accuse the homeowners, Charles and Cathy Taylor, of allowing widespread underage drinking, providing marijuana and obstructing justice by telling kids to hide.

The Taylors would not comment, but their lawyer, Russell Bickert, disputes the authorities' version. He said the couple didn't know teens were drinking, didn't have marijuana and didn't hide anyone. The Taylors are to meet ... with a Passaic County prosecutor to discuss a plea deal.

Police recall the following details:

As the first cruiser pulled up, most of the partygoers took off, hopping fences and diving into the woods, scrambling for cover so fast that they left behind winter coats despite nearly freezing temperatures, Officers—who would eventually conclude that about 75 kids had been at the party—called for backup. As some followed the fleeing kids, others interviewed whoever was caught, including one girl who gouged her hand so badly on a fence that she needed 15 stitches at St. Joseph's Wayne Hospital.

Some teens had alcohol on their breath. Some appeared drunk. Several told police straight out that they'd been drinking at the party.

Despite all the commotion outside the house, ever more parents kept pulling up to drop off their sons and daughters.

Sgt. Anthony Padula knocked on the door. It was opened by Charles Taylor, the 51-year-old father of the host. "What's going on?" Padula asked.

Taylor said his son had "some of his friends over."

"Some?" thought Padula.

Through the door, the officer saw opened beer cans scattered across the floor. Turning back to Taylor, he said: "We have a problem."

"Cluelessness" Abounds

Substance abuse researchers say the prevalence of teen drinking, while down from a decade ago, remains stubbornly high. It is particularly acute among white, affluent teens. Nationwide, about 30 percent of white and Hispanic high school students report having had five or more drinks in a row at least once in the past month, twice the rate of blacks.

But for every kid hauled into police headquarters and every party broken up, countless others slip under the radar of police—and parents.

"There's a profound level of cluelessness," said Andy Yeager, a Park Ridge High School counselor and the point man for substance abuse education in Bergen County. "The parents of ninth-graders say, 'It's not my kid.' And the parents of 10th- through 12th-graders say, 'Oh, I did it at their age. At least it's beer, not heroin.'"

Perhaps, then, it's not surprising that alcohol is so easy to get. Beyond fake IDs and willing older friends, many teenagers sneak from their parents' liquor cabinet—or get their party drinks directly from Mom or Dad.

"Sometimes parents will get us, like, 30 bottles of beer, because they know kids will drink anyway and they'd rather have them home than risk their being on the road," said Lauren, a sophomore who lives in a Pascack Valley town.

Other parents refuse to provide it, but look the other way.

"I'd say half the time, parents are home, but they know not to interfere or pop their heads in," said one 11th-grader at a Bergen County private school who has her pick of parties every weekend. "They stay in another part of the house."

Still others don't see what the problem is—and even challenge the police.

"We have parents who say, 'Don't you have anything better to do?'" Tenafly juvenile officer Detective Tim O'Reilly said. "Or 'They're just drinking. What's the big deal?' Or 'Why are you picking on my kid?'"

Back at the Taylors'

Stepping inside, Padula asked Charles Taylor if he had been home the whole evening. Taylor said yes. Padula wondered if Taylor had misheard him, He asked again.

"You were here when all this, the party, was going on?"

Taylor repeated that he and his wife, Cathy, had spent the entire evening in the room adjacent to the party, according to police, some of whom knew the Taylors. They were respected members of the community—he a letter carrier and Eagle Scout, she a nursery school teacher and Cub Scout leader.

As police fanned out through the house, they saw open cases of beer and garbage bags of empty beer cans and bottles of rum, vodka and whiskey, as well as a plastic Ziploc bag of marijuana.

Suddenly, a woman appeared at the front door to claim her panicked daughter, who had just called from an attic closet.

Detective David Parenta hollered upstairs, "There's a narcotics detection canine in the house! Anybody upstairs better come down now, 'cause the dog's coming up!"

A dozen kids shot out of the attic, including the Taylors' 15-year-old son, Parenta said.

Police rounded up 40 teens, 31 of them just 14 or 15 years old. Some were picked up a good quarter-mile away, outside the Foodtown and Belmont Bakery, shivering in shirt sleeves.

Carload by carload, police hauled them in to take statements. Soon the little stationhouse was jammed—boys in headquarters, girls in the courtroom. Some kids smirked. Some sat somberly. Some cried.

Near midnight, as the questioning wore on, one 15-year-old boy suddenly threw up on the carpet by the dispatcher, then passed out. He was taken to St. Joseph's Wayne Hospital. Diagnosis: alcohol poisoning.

Parents lined up outside, waiting. Some thanked police. Others grumbled it was ridiculous their kids were carted in for such a minor transgression.

It wasn't until almost 3 a.m. that the last kid trudged out of the police station.

"I Lied to My Parents"

There's no doubt parents are in a bind.

Public health experts, including the National Academy of Sciences, have lambasted the alcohol industry for aggressively marketing to minors. Critics point to the proliferation of "alco-pops," the sweet-tasting, flavored alcoholic beverages popular among teen girls, such as Mike's Hard Lemonade. They dismiss the industry's claims of innocence, pointing out that in 2004, alcohol was advertised on the 15 television shows with the largest teen audiences. Long-term studies have shown that the more youth are exposed to alcohol ads, the more likely they are to drink and binge.

Then, of course, parents have to contend with the nature of teenagers.

"You drink because it makes you more relaxed, so kids will like you more," said one Park Ridge High School sophomore. "And if you're young, like in ninth grade, and you go to a junior or senior party and you drink, then they'll think you're cool and they might let you be one of them."

Teens boast about their clever deceptions. One Glen Rock boy admitted to setting off in his car to convince his parents he wouldn't be drinking, then stashing it nearby so he wouldn't have to drive far when he was drunk. Another teenager, to dupe her parents into believing she wasn't out drinking, persuaded a stranger at the Ridgewood movie theater to give up his ticket stub so she had an alibi.

"I lied to my parents about everything," a 17-year-old from Leonia said. "I'd say it wasn't a party, or that there would be no alcohol or drugs, or that the parents would be there. I would say that I didn't drink much anyway because I didn't like it. It was a total lie. I was drinking almost every weekend."

Put it all together and parents are left with agonizing questions: If I punish my child when she admits to drinking, won't she be less truthful the next time? If I don't set consequences, won't she think I condone underage drinking? Isn't it better to allow my child to drink with friends at home with me nearby than somewhere less supervised?

Some parents are so afraid of their child's disapproval that they ask someone else to play the heavy. Police in several towns have been astonished by parents who drop off kids at parties, then rat out the soirees to police.

"They won't say no to their kids," Ringwood Police Chief Bernard Lombardo said. "We say, wait a minute, you just dropped your kid off there!"

Mothers Against Drunk Driving preaches "zero tolerance," but many parents worry such prohibitions are unrealistic and likely to backfire.

Although Ann Martino of Glen Rock does not allow her 17-year-old, Jill, to invite friends over to drink, she does let Jill have an occasional glass of wine at dinner. She assumes Jill drinks when she's with friends but trusts it's not to excess because Jill is a good student and reliable.

"If they're going to make a mistake, I'd like them to learn while I'm around," said Martino, mother of three, "I can't be that on top of her that she's going to be smothered. I have to give her some rope. She has not disappointed me."

Did Police Overreact?

Three days after the North Haledon party, the Taylors were charged with serving alcohol to minors, possession of marijuana with intent to distribute, 33 counts of endangering the welfare of children, and obstruction of government function for allegedly hiding kids in the attic. Their son was charged with disorderly conduct, possession of marijuana and drug paraphernalia and intent to distribute drugs.

"They're absolutely not guilty," said their attorney.

Charles Taylor was put on paid administrative leave from the Wyckoff post office, which is awaiting the outcome. Cathy Taylor was suspended from the North Haledon Cooperative Nursery School. Their son's case is pending in the juvenile system.

In the days after the party, some town residents complained to Mayor Randy George that police overreacted. But George, father of three teenagers and a 20-year-old, is philosophical.

"A parent makes a bad decision and it affects more than just them," he said. "This time, thank God, no one was badly hurt, but what if something more had happened? How can parents say the police were being ridiculous when our officers were trying to keep those kids safe? Kids who are the single most important part of a parent's life?

"I don't know if anyone has learned their lesson from this, but I'd sure like to think so. It's only when we all band together and realize the seriousness of the situation that we can change it."

Drinking Is Both the Problem and the Solution for an Alcoholic

Chris Volkmann and Toren Volkmann

Toren Volkmann abused alcohol from his early teenage years until he suffered an emotional breakdown at the age of twenty-four while serving in the Peace Corps. From Binge to Blackout details the circumstances that led up to Toren's breakdown, his detoxification, and his rehabilitation. While Toren retraces the steps of his steady decline into alcoholism, his mother, Chris, relates how she overcame denial to become an active participant in her son's recovery process. In the following excerpt, Toren recounts his personally destructive relationship with alcohol during college and in the months following his graduation. While Volkmann comes to realize that he is an alcoholic, he finds that drinking alcohol is the only way to counteract the debilitating physical symptoms of withdrawal, including nausea, muscle tremors, sleeplessness, and anxiety. But he also acknowledges that alcohol controls his life to the point that he can barely function in social situations.

Paraguay, May 21, 2003. A long night of drinking used to make me tired . . . now it makes me stay up and shake. I'm an alcoholic. I guess drinking like an alcoholic for about eight or nine years was part of the problem. Luckily, it was fun as hell.

Now what? Cocaine? How can I find a new identity when I used to drink mine by the fluid ounce and then turn around and juggle reality?

I thought the problem with being an alcoholic was you just drank a lot. I did that just fine and things were great. No one ever said, "Dude, you're gonna start losing your money, your memory and, above all, your longevity and tolerance. . ." as if just being shit-faced and happy every night weren't enough, ". . . and when you stop a mean bender you're going to be a fevering, shaky, paranoid halfwit for a day or two who can't think, sleep, relax, or even eat until withdrawals are over. . . ." That page of my D.A.R.E. [Drug Abuse Resistance Education] book must have been ripped out, right after the one part I do remember that said the bad guys always had fun and got all the chicks.

Realization Sets In

I used to be able to handle the worst of hangovers, wear it like a soldier wore a uniform, or drink it off. I could deal with hellacious sleeplessness from drinking for a day or through the night, maybe ending up in some random bed and still charging through class, ball practice, or family happenings like the dark angel that I was . . . even the torrential blackouts that would be reported or random acts of split personality. My friends and I always gave ourselves alternate drinking names (mine was Poren), as a joke, saying, "So and so did that, not me." It was nothing to be ashamed of in the glory days. Things are changing, and what I once thirsted for and sucked on with the finest appreciation, shared with the warmest of friends in the best and most f---ed-up times, is beginning to scare me.

The problem isn't controlling my urge to drink; it's what happens to me now when I drink. (Twenty-four pack, where are you?) What was once all benefit and reward—raging parties, boring conversation turned into passionate arguments, blaring music and endless cigarettes, slurring exchanges of understanding (or even unfaithful or unwarranted kisses)—now seems to be packaged with much more unpredictability. I now have a harder time controlling how much I drink and how drunk I get.

Even more disturbing are the terrible physical reactions, depending on the amount of alcohol I consumed and my eventual detox. This is the big problem. During detox, inside the unsettled body, a nervous and sometimes nauseous sense begins . . . an anxiety and almost a fear, like being too alone. You see yourself and everything differently. Like a sudden collapse of the stock market in your brain and every single nerve ending throughout your body wants to turn inside out and puke out some unidentifiable pain or itch. You sweat, and you sweat increasingly when you let unreasonable thoughts trick you into feeling like whatever you are thinking must be true, like for example, "this is normal." "this will never end," "I deserve this," or "hhhhmm . . . maybe another drink will solve the problem."

Each summer, I returned from college in San Diego to my home in Olympia [Washington], to live with my folks and work by day as a groundskeeper. But really, I lived for the weekends, and everything worked out perfectly that way. I would go up to Seattle and rock all weekend, hardly eating and just shooting the shit (loving it always), cracking beers from the early morning and turning over what was remaining from the previous night. The weekends were endless parties, fiascos, adventures. And always intoxicating.

A Vicious Cycle

That last summer at home, I grew to dread Monday mornings at work, and sometimes Tuesdays, too. It wasn't due to a headache or hating the job. I liked being outside and listening to all the jack-offs on talk radio with their big opinions and constant advertising. But more and more, I would feel exhausted. Sunday or Monday nights I would find myself in bed at nine or ten p.m., knowing that I may not get to sleep until four, five, or six a.m. My legs would cramp sometimes, or ache, depending on how bad it was, or how much I had drunk. I'd have sweaty, sudden convulsions just as my body began to relax or fall asleep. I would be scared to fall asleep and would lie awake frightened, having no clue what to do, in total dread until it would finally subside enough to let me sleep. *Hell.* I tried to think it was normal, but I knew something was up. Little did I know it was the start of what I would slowly come to realize was part of my reality. It was my penance after coming off another celebratory binge. Starting out subtly as uneasiness, anxiousness, and sleeplessness, these reactions slowly progressed over the last two years of college.

The first time I ever noticed that I had the shakes and didn't attribute it to lack of food was in 2000, my sophomore year of college . . . I was not even twenty-one years old. I was trying to fix a tangled cassette. Unfortunately, my hand was vibrating, so I gave myself some wine and was to enjoy the tape along with the rest of the wine, after both problems were fixed. Buzzed and horrified, I called my brother and recounted to him what had happened, as if I'd just had my first wet dream or some other eventual rite of passage to manhood. He was unsurprised, if I remember correctly, and I think he more or less welcomed me to the club or alluded to the idea of "Where have you been?" That made me feel better, as did the rest of the boxed wine.

I made it through college just fine and, from what I remember, it was the time of my life. I have a lot of really screwed-up pictures, a black book, and valuable friendships to prove it. I became very disheartened with my difficult routine by the end, though. My senior year was awfully tough. Getting blitzed every weekend was amazing, and returning to the dorms on campus, backpedaling, was always a challenge . . . to say the least.

I used to tell people, the few who understood, how my ridiculous schedule went:

Schizophrenic Monday: Inferior to myself, self-worth plummeting, no schoolwork, too preoccupied and on edge . . . easily startled by common things, vulnerable, and self-esteem at negative ten.

Worry Tuesday: Still fevering, blankly staring at TV, wondering how I am gonna magically execute all that reading, classes, papers, exams (brilliantly done in the end, I must add).

Whatever Wednesday: How much I really drank last weekend = how I function this day.

Productive Thursday: Back on track and kicking ass, do it all, I *am* school.

F---ing Friday: Sense of humor fully restored, all energy and in gear . . . just in time to start the cycle all over again-. . .pattern here?????????????

This gave me about two or three days of productivity. So on Fridays I would delve into bliss, oblivion, carelessness, and a state of being that defied concern. One that was mostly impossible for the average student or peer. Satisfactorily saturated, self-sufficient, and in need of nothing more than my friends and my cheap booze (211, forties, ice beers, or maybe some other high-class malt liquor), I was set. I would drink the half-empty leftover beers (wounded soldiers) and I'd wonder about the party-goers who had gone home early, "What was their problem?" Well, whatever those people did, they didn't seem to catch *my* disease. It must be something toward the bottom of the drink that did it. Anyway, I had the best of times. Simplicity—lots of rocking music, companionship, and drinking games (Quarters, Keg Stands, Beirut, Kings, and Dr. Kilabrew). Done deal. No bars or girl chasing, just laughs, craziness, and comfort. Where was the problem? (See Schizophrenic Monday.)

At this point in my life, I wasn't sure if this was a disease or not (they say it is). I chose it and loved it. Now if I choose to drink like I did before, the symptoms that ensue are surely my fault. I am simply struggling with the aftermath of the next good time that I want to have. Why does detox have to exist and be sooooo painful, making me struggle to talk, and even lose my sense of humor? These are the functions alcohol usually eases for people, but now the results are the opposite. It has me totally puzzled and unsure how to explain it, mainly to the ones I care about, and also the ones who may be alcoholics, as well.

Drinking Is What I Do Best

After I graduated college in the summer of 2002, I moved up to Seattle to live with some old friends from high school. To save words, I again put into action what I did best. I drank— almost every day. No more school, a bad job market, and man, it was perfect. Even better, there were World Cup soccer matches on TV every night to keep me wasted until five in the morning. *Gooaaallll!!!!!*

Eventually I started landscaping, and I still went hard every night, partying. It didn't seem to matter. I woke up with vigor and readiness. I packed my lunch, and then would get stuck in traffic with my music and a cigarette, knowing that I could work, get money, and go home to good friends and drinks. And those were my summer week*days*. The weekends were ten times better, with girls and parties, concerts, or occasional visits to Olympia. There wasn't a care in the world, and I never had to come down.

Sometimes I would start to come down—maybe I didn't drink much the night before or had an appointment or family dinner. I snuck by without drinking or even nursing a few down, and I'd start slipping into alcohol withdrawal. In these moments, with a wet and hot/cold forehead, I'd find it difficult to focus on the task at hand, like remembering that I was supposed to bring something to the car or not knowing what I had just talked about with someone for ten minutes. My inability to recall details was very annoying, and the further into withdrawal I would get, the more frustrations turned into fears, anxieties, loss of confidence and purpose, and even worse, a disappearing sense of humor. This is the shit that makes up your personality, and when it suddenly starts to change or disintegrate, it is freaky and no fun. It seems totally beyond control—purely physical.

The summer ended with the whole crew of friends seeming to have graduated, changed locations, or split up to travel or whatever. I had signed myself up to go with the U.S. government for two years, hopefully to South America. It was not to fight in the armed forces but to serve as a volunteer in the Peace Corps. This gave me several months to kill, and I would almost literally do this.

Binge Drinking in Vegas

I spent the better part of September and October of 2002 in Las Vegas, and at times on road trips to the coast—mainly to touch base with all my study buddies, right? My biggest plan was to spend time with my two brothers, who worked in Vegas, and visit friends from school in San Diego. I have tried to recount and distinguish the nights and different trips to San Diego, and it is almost impossible. Invariably we had a blast and I was losing great chunks of each night, either corresponding to (1) how much fun we had, or (2) how much of a jackass I (Poren) may have been.

I drank every night in Vegas, too. It was great. We raged through the casinos, walked down the crowded strip with our sleazy malt liquors and cheap half racks, almost rubbing in the fact that we could do such a thing in front of such "classy" gambling folks. On our better nights, we would then find ourselves at the trashy Gold Spike Casino, giggling and doing penny slots super early in the morning. Luckily, we knew gambling was another issue we didn't need. Besides, every time you give the 7-Eleven cashier ninety-nine cents, you know you get a twenty-four-ounce can of Steel Reserve malt liquor that'll get you just that much more wasted. Where's the gamble in that?

Soon after, I went to Oaxaca, Mexico, to study Spanish in preparation for my upcoming service in South America. En route, on a layover in Houston one morning, I took desperate measures to put off the impending withdrawal that I knew would be coming after five months of continuous drinking. I made a quick stop at the airport bar to down three screwdrivers (orange juice and vodka). It was worth the twenty-dollar bar tab because it bought me some time before the madness of my detox would set in. It helped me get through the air travel to Mexico City, and later a bus trip to Oaxaca without sweats, memory breakdowns, and the general ineptness that occur during withdrawal. Not that I wanted to see this as a problem or anything.

Dealing with Severe Withdrawal

Upon arrival in Mexico, I was met with the harshest of withdrawals, which magnified everything I have previously described. I spent two solid nights in a hotel, clawing at bedsheets, taking cold showers, and only going out to find water and a banana (hoping not to be noticed or to have to talk while aiming to remember where my room was with all my stuff). After those two days I proceeded to "recover," and basically stayed away from alcohol all but two or three times in the following weeks. The clarity was quick in coming, comforting, and surprisingly easy. I knew my reality was scary.

From this point on, I think something hit me and began telling me "I can never, at least physically, go back to the way I was." I knew that, not just financially, but physically, I would pay for every drink or intoxicatingly good time I would have. Meeting my family for Christmas in Mexico after eight weeks of language class (and some travel, with a few slipups, we'll say) was perfect—a chance to say good-bye before leaving for the Peace Corps for two years. I showed up sober and beyond any chance of withdrawal. My bros pulled in from Vegas with carry-on bags under their eyes and the scent of a great night on their breath. I was amazed and jealous at the same time. But they didn't seem in too bad shape. How? I couldn't have done that.

The first two days or so with the family were great. I remember sitting with one of my brothers at a table at sunset, watching my uncle and cousins surf-fishing in the shallow waves. We were talking, smiling, sharing a beer, and savoring a perfect moment. How things should be.

How could the situation change?

Sobriety Does Not Last Long

"Paging Dr. Toren Volkmann. Please report to your own personal disaster called alcoholism—the tremors, sweats, and antisocial symptoms will be right with you." All I needed to do was start drinking.

Sure enough, after a few hard drinks (tequila that tasted like it had been made in a bathtub), the process began to start. Eventually, the paranoid, confused, intoxicated *me* showed up, teetering on the edge of withdrawal. This side of detox is the one that turns a regular conversation into a task. Even if it is with the closest of friends, it doesn't matter. Although they might not notice, inside me is another whole world of pain. The anxiety and difficulty that exists depends on the alcohol levels in my body—either previously consumed or in deficit.

After Mexico, I had one last stint in San Diego before my final goodbye with my brothers in Las Vegas. I don't remember shit for the most part, and even skipped out on seeing some of my most important friends because I was too gone to really care or make an effort to contact some of them. As it turned out, thanks to a stolen disposable camera and Satan himself, some pictures revealed that I did actually see a few of them. Silly ol' me.

That last morning in San Diego I found myself driving to Vegas in a borrowed car with a gal I didn't know too well. We stopped once, and talked about the same number of times. Although sleepless, I knew that my good old withdrawals wouldn't let me relax, so I was confident I would not fall asleep at the wheel. I even let the same CD repeat over and over because I felt too sick and stupid to suggest that we put in another.

The more days in a row I would drink, the more easily these symptoms would surface, and the more intensely they hindered my normal relaxed style of thinking and way of interacting with others. It really started to steal my enthusiasm, my aura, and my soul. I probably could have looked into a mirror and seen the back wall at times, things seemed so bad. This was not the life I'd ordered.

The Problem and the Solution

During my final Las Vegas days, I kept a steady supply in me and generally had a good time. The previous months studying in Mexico had made me realize that my drinking situation was worse than I thought. Drinking now emerged as both my problem and my solution. In opportune moments I think I tried to hint to both my brothers that I was bothered by some of the shit that it was doing to me. (They knew what "it" was and what I was talking about. They're my f---ing brothers. But maybe they didn't.) What I was trying to tell them surely didn't come out clearly. In fact, nothing came out conclusively because I didn't want to say it. If the first step to beating the problem is admitting it or accepting it, I guess I just didn't want to beat anything quite yet. Why the hell did it have to be so bad all of a sudden?

Leaving Las Vegas was maybe the low point to this day, in my new "dialogue" with alcohol [things got much lower after writing this]. On the floor that last morning, I woke up all too early—which often happens when the body starts losing its normal equilibrium of alcohol—lying next to a girl I really cared for. We may have actually had sex the previous night (if

I could only piece together a few simple clues with some certainty). The fact is that I totally slept with her. I was leaving for two years and I knew we should talk about it. Experiencing withdrawals, uncomfortable and unable to sleep, I tried to act asleep to avoid the whole situation, which should have been a memorable good-bye. I didn't know what the hell to say and I felt like crap. It only made me feel worse hiding my problem from her and sweating out the hours that should have been shared between friends.

With few hours left in Vegas, my problem was worsening without drinks (I didn't want to reek of alcohol when my mom picked me up at the airport), and I had to tear down whatever I wanted from our tastelessly covered walls and pack for my departure and upcoming disappearance. My brothers did half of the work for me, I was so worthless. Good-byes are always difficult, but what ensued was terrible. I look back on it with sadness and regret. I tried but couldn't even smile or appreciate our final moments, or express the joy, the love I had for my brothers and my friends. I was too lost in fevers, trembles, and general ineptness, and I felt like they all could see right through it. I was out of my mind. I was scared to leave, scared of what was happening inside me. It was killing me and was all wrong for no reason. My life was supposed to be great.

Eventually, I boarded a plane home to Seattle, my body in pain, shaking, and my legs aching. Behind me, all the way, a baby shrieked as if to express my exact state of being while magnifying it at the same time. I could barely tolerate to sit, stand, think—to live. My mom picked me up at the airport and I played it off legit. It was a tough ride home, trying to read letters about my Peace Corps assignment in South America, making normal conversation that made no sense to me, only wanting to disappear.

Experiencing Feelings of Worthlessness

I had two days to "relax" and a night of nonsleep, like so many previous nights during those wild Seattle summers, before the symptoms slowly subsided. I didn't even try to start packing for South America, knowing any brainless attempt would just provoke sweaty confusion and stress. I was worthless. I could barely explain photos of my language school and travels in Mexico to my parents, because I was still so affected by the recovery from that latest binge I had put myself through. Why was it suddenly so hard?

In my hometown in early January 2003, with a bit more time before leaving, I wiggled my way out of seeing most of my old high school friends and drinking buddies. I wanted to be sane in my final days before departing for the Peace Corps in order to prepare myself. Yes, by then I had learned what happens when I drink, but it wasn't over yet. Being sober, I was able to find myself and deal with fears of leaving the country for two years with logic and confidence in myself. But departing to another continent by no means left my problem behind.

The question is: What do I do now? How can I make this work? What I can't help but wonder is whether all those famous (dead) rock stars, winos on the streets, or some of my best friends have experienced these same types of things or are experiencing them now? Maybe they just never said so or aren't admitting it. Maybe what I experience is much different from others. But I can't imagine anyone bearing the internal hell that I feel as a result of hard drinking and continuing on without letting others know. How did I not ever hear about this side of alcohol and withdrawal? For me, the silence is over and it is time to start looking for answers. I am also looking for the right cliché to end this—bottoms up!!

A Student Recalls Binge Drinking in Canada

Koren Zailckas

Koren Zailckas took her first drink of alcohol before entering high school. Over the course of the next decade, she engaged in a lifestyle of alcohol abuse that is not uncommon for countless teenagers in America today. Her personal experiences span the entire life cycle of alcohol abuse, from sneaking drinks out of her parents' liquor cabinet, to wild teenage parties, to binge drinking in college, and finally to recovery. In the following excerpt reprinted from her memoir Smashed: Story of a Drunken Girlhood. *Zailckas reminisces about the events surrounding a formal dance that was organized at a hotel in Canada by her college sorority chapter. Although some four hours away from Syracuse University where Zailckas attended school, Canada is a popular destination for American underage drinkers because the country's minimum age for buying and consuming alcohol is eighteen or nineteen, depending on the province. Zailckas recalls how she and her friends bought a vast amount of alcohol and drank to excess at the hotel. Their actions, the author writes, led to drug abuse, vomiting from binge drinking, and a near date rape experience in her hotel room after the dance.*

A formal is like a high school prom, but with an open bar and no chaperones. Most sororities at S.U. [Syracuse University] have them, and mostly at resorts in Canada, where across the border just four hours away, the legal drinking age is eighteen. Everyone spends the night in a three-star hotel, doing their best impression of Led Zeppelin at the Continen-

Koren Zailckas, *Smashed: Story of a Drunken Girlhood*, New York: Ebury, 2005. Copyright © Koren Zailckas, 2005. All rights reserved. In US reproduced by permission of Viking Penguin, a division of Penguin Group (USA) Inc. In UK reprinted by permission of Random House Group Ltd. (UK).

tal Hyatt by kicking over nightstands, putting cigarette burns in hotel towels, and disrupting things enough to make other guests file formal complaints.

No sister wants to go alone, but asking a date is a big deal because you have to share a hotel room with him.

I end up inviting a boy named Milton who lives on Hannah's floor in Sadler Hall. We met a month earlier, in the dorm bathroom, where I was getting sick after a night of downing 7&7s [a mixed drink of whiskey and lemon-lime soda]. The room felt as damp as a sea cave, and Milton found me in one of the stalls, where I was drifting to sleep with my cheek on the toilet seat and hugging the bowl like a life preserver. In memory, he was a giant sea beast that latched on to me, kissing me right there on the tiles without even bothering to help me up from my space among the stray wads of toilet paper. I hadn't resisted. Unmoored as I was, I was happy for rescue.

I don't really *like* Milton, but I don't dislike him, which is the standard by which I measure the boys with whom I drink. I figure bringing him will be better than not going at all, or going stag, in which case I'd be sure to end up alone in a corner, taking shots, while everyone else snuggled into slow dances. Since I haven't ever been to a formal, I don't know that boys interpret the invite as an open invitation for sex, on account of both the open bar and the hotel room. If I'd known, I never would have asked.

Milton and I hitch a ride up to the Canadian side of Niagara Falls with Hannah, who also joined Zeta, and her date, Perry, a platonic friend she went to high school with. It is the slow, awkward drive of people who don't know what to talk about. We wheel up Interstate 81, past the army base in Watertown and through the Thousand Islands. Hannah fiddles with the radio. Perry folds and unfolds the map. Milton says over and over that he should have brought his stash of pot. When we get to the border, a customs officer in a glass booth waves us through, despite the fact that when he asks what country we are citizens of, Perry says "Scranton, Pennsylvania."

We park the car in front of the first packaged-goods store we spot, and skitter through the aisles like contestants on *Supermarket Sweep*, amassing bottles of rum and tequila, plus a thirty-pack of beer and the stubby Canadian cigarettes called Players. It should be a thrill to be able to buy booze legally, but for some reason, I still feel sheepish, like I'm doing something wrong. I hand a few bills to Milton and let him carry my share to the counter, where a bald man knowingly rings them up.

Drinking Legally in Canada

By the time we get to the hotel, most of the sisters have already checked in. They are moving the elevator up and down, bursting in and out of rooms holding beer bottles. There are Zetas smoking a joint in the lounge chairs beside the indoor pool, and more sitting at the hotel bar like birds on a wire, picking through peanut bowls and chatting with the bartender while he pulls back the lever of the beer tap. It's the first time I've ever checked into a hotel without my parents, and I'm unsure what to do at the horseshoe-shaped front desk, where a clerk in a hunter-green blazer hands me my room key card.

Hannah and I have arranged to have adjoining rooms on the ground floor. Mine has two double beds because I don't feel wholly comfortable bunking with Milton.

The Party Begins

The rooms have sliding glass doors that open onto a small bay, and Hannah and I jog outside without our coats on to marvel at its half-frozen finish. We sit on the broad wooden railing that divides the lawn from the water, holding bottles of Labatt's [beer] in our laps and sighing in the dippy, satisfied way the situation seems to call for. The air around us is smoky before we even light a cigarette. It's not dark yet, but we can see the moon, as though by mistake. Hannah says the clouds make its edges look serrated, like a bottle cap.

Back in the hotel room, Hannah and I drink while Perry snaps pictures. We lie under the bed's stiff paisley comforter with our backs against the headboard, like a married couple watching the eleven o'clock news. Between us are an ashtray, a bottle of Captain Morgan coconut rum, and the tiny juice glasses from the hotel bathroom that we've been using to take shots.

After a few deep dips into the bottle, I locate the inner button that can take me off mute mode. I come up with a point of conversation. I ask everyone, "What was the last ludicrous thing you did when you were drunk?" I find out that Milton passed out in his closet. Hannah accidentally penciled in her eyebrows with red lip-liner in a bar's dark bathroom. Perry peed into his refrigerator's vegetable drawer during a drunken sleepwalk.

People seem to visit our room in sixes. Girls I pledged with come by to rap on the door, as does Maya, as well as boys in rumpled dress shirts who turn out to be other sisters' dates. Everyone is chain-smoking Players and posing for pictures, asking for beer and offering pot, until our standard-sized room starts to feel like a bank with Perry playing the teller. Since he bought most of the booze, he supervises the deposits and withdrawals.

The whole time, I stay curled up in the sheets with the rum bottle, feeling too gratified to leave it. Around the room, other sisters are bear-hugging a plastic pink bong or nuzzling drinks, and it occurs to me that this formal is like our honeymoon, like the ravenous periods of early love. In Canada, we can hardly believe we can drink legally, the way newlyweds can hardly grasp that they're married. We shut ourselves up in our rooms, consummating our lust. We consume room service, our drinks, and our dates. Each taste makes our union feel a little more real.

I know I'm starting to get drunk because I can feel my eyes turn to marbles in my head. I love that about alcohol. It has a way of making my whole face relax, the way I imagine a facial must. When I'm this slack, I wonder why I always feel so tense to begin with, why I walk around with my cheeks pulled so tight they look hollow, why my mouth is always drawn tight, into a constipated-looking little *o*.

I once heard someone use *copacetic* as a slang term for "drunk," and I thought *That's me*. With a buzz on, I'm first-rate. Alcohol is my wood sealant. When I'm painted, nothing can penetrate my essence. My best friend can call me *bitch*. The boy who is brushing my thigh with the back of his hand can tell me I'm only pretty when he's drunk. In the moment, these sentiments just bead up and roll off me.

I don't even mind when Milton crosses the room to smooth my hair, as though he cared about me.

"We're Such Goddamn Americans"

Sometime later, we run out of booze, and Hannah, Perry, and I go to buy more at what we don't realize is a gigantic, fine-wine store. The bottles that line the shelves from floor to ceiling are far too good for the likes of us. I tramp through the rows of labels from Portugal, Argentina, and New Zealand—all the regions I'm too uncultivated to know—with the mania of Augustus Gloop in the chocolate room [in *Charlie and the Chocolate Factory*].

It occurs to me that an hour has passed since my last drink, and my buzz has begun soft-pedaling. I am still drunk, but I cannot be *just*-drunk. Just-drunk will not gut my head of its worries. Just-drunk will not swat away my misgivings about Milton, anxieties that are whirring around me when I'm alone with him, like so many insects. I need a bottle of something sweet and potent to perk me back up to a state of past-gone. Champagne will do the trick. Cheap champagne, which is both romantic and lethal, will hit me like a crime of passion. I think it can help me behead myself.

Hannah is in the back of the store, inspecting the coolers stocked with chilled Korbel, as if she has read my mind. But when I approach her to help select a fat green bottle from the cooler's shelf, she doubles over with her hands on her knees, and starts dry heaving.

I'm able to grab her under one arm, and get her out of the store before the store owner has to run for a mop. The door chimes, and the cold Canadian air hits us hard and blue. I tug Hannah just around the corner of the storefront, where we're out of the cashier's view, and I hold her blonde curls while she throws up on the sidewalk. I grit my teeth when I hear the splashing sound vomit makes when it hits concrete.

We're standing on the edge of the town's main street, and traffic is heavy. Every few minutes, a car whizzes by. The drivers, mostly men, lean against their car horns, and the blares are mocking. Hannah wipes her mouth with the pink sleeve of her sweater and says, "We're such goddamn Americans."

Binge Drinking Takes Stamina

When we make it back to the Crown Princess Hotel, Hannah is still down for the count, so Perry and I haul her to bed and go about the business of changing for the dance.

In what will become a mythic recovery, Hannah will wake up stone-sober two hours later, wriggle into her black satin gown, loop her hair into an updo, and come downstairs to resume drinking. As college continues, we will all build up this level of stamina, which may be the truest measure of excess. Sorority sisters who are drunk enough to have eyes swiveling around in their heads will learn to tickle their throats with their fingers, hurl, and reel back to the party to pick up drinking where they left off.

In spite of the scene at the liquor store, I still managed to net a bottle of champagne. Perry pops the cork out the sliding glass door, where it cracks like a gunshot. Milton has been lost for hours, and I'm glad because I don't have to think about him. I can just drink champagne from a bathroom glass with Perry, whom I feel comfortable with on account that he isn't my love interest, or even Hannah's.

Each sip of champagne tastes like honey. I love the whispering sound its bubbles make, as though the drink itself is trying to tell me something. After a few glasses, I am too unsteady on my feet to slip into my new floor-length gold dress without stepping on the hem and half-falling over.

Getting ready is the most challenging part about formal weekend. After five hours of pre-parties, a mascara brush is just as dangerous to operate as heavy machinery, and when we develop the film from our disposable cameras, everyone's makeup looks like Tammy Faye's. High on champagne, my biggest challenge is scooping out my suitcase. After twenty minutes of pawing through my clothes, I still can't locate two high heels. When the time comes, I go downstairs to the ballroom wearing Milton's rubber flip-flops.

Budgeting for Booze, Not Food

The dance itself is the least interesting part of the weekend. For a few hours, there's an open bar, and we drink screwdrivers garnished with orange wedges through tiny plastic straws. As a sorority, we were too cheap to have the event catered, so the white tablecloths are covered with confetti but no food, and our empty stomachs make us even more drunk. On a banquet table are a few cheese plates, sticky glasses that are half-full or half-empty of cocktails, and ashtrays smoking with forgotten, unmashed cigarettes. The deejay we hired was detained at customs, so there's a Canadian one, spinning the culturally offensive music that's usually reserved for terrorist interrogations.

Zeta's president requests Crosby, Stills, and Nash, which is something that someone will do at every formal henceforth.

When it comes on, the sisters make a ring on the dance floor, linking arms and slurring the words to "Our House." I join in, wrapping my arms around the synthetic material of two people's dress waists, and chirping about how life used to be hard, but now everything is easy because of Zeta. I tilt my head against the sister standing next to me and let my eyes well up. The words zing out of me because I don't yet know what a Greek myth they are.

The rest of the night flickers on like a movie that you watch while you're nodding off to sleep, and catch only pieces of. The vodka I drank in the ballroom omits some scenes, but I manage to pay attention to the important events in the plot. Milton materializes during a slow song, when he tows me onto the dance floor by my elbow, and I let him twirl me a few times before I flip-flop back to the bar. Perry finds a piano in a hallway and thumps out a labored rendition of something truly campy, maybe "You Are So Beautiful." Someone snaps a picture of me standing beside him, listening, with one hand on the piano's lid. In it, my eyes look blank, and my skin is as white as chicken meat.

Sometime after midnight, Hannah and I get the idea to climb onto the slick roof of a ferry that is tied up in the bay. The red letters painted on the ferry's side read SEA FOX, though Hannah keeps calling it SEX FOX. We plunk ourselves down on top of the boat's bridge, smoking a joint and shouting "All aboard" as loud as we can, to see if the ice will toss our voices back in an echo.

Sometime after that, I slide back through the door of my hotel room and pass out alone in the sheets.

Playing Dead

The room is as dark as first darkness, the way only hotel rooms can be. In my sleep I can hear the old-fashioned clock on the nightstand flip its numbers. I know I will not be able to sleep soundly here, knowing Milton still remains at large, and that he might tear through the door at any minute with his plastic key. Beyond that, I can never fully doze off when I am this loaded with hard liquor. Vodka, especially, lulls me into a state of delirious half-sleep, in which I talk and laugh out loud.

I'm lying on my side, facing the blank white wall, when Milton comes in. I can tell he is wasted by the way he falters onto the bed, clasping me from behind and wiping his wet mouth on my collarbone. I can feel his penis pressed between my shoulder blades like I'm being robbed at knifepoint.

I feel stalled between consciousness and sleep, the way I used to on the mornings when my mother used to wake me up for high school. In my dreams, I'm saying *Go away go away go away go away*, but in reality I'm not sure I'm exhaling a damn word. My jaw feels too stiff to speak through.

Milton is kneading my rib cage like a ball of dough, hard enough to make me glad I'm this drunk—otherwise, his hands would hurt. Tomorrow, when I'm inspecting the bruises, I'll think I should have quoted the poet Milton, who said, "He who overcomes by force overcomes by half his foe." But in the moment, I can't think at all. Liquor has strained my mind. It has exhausted my heart. My only defense is my vacancy. I hope if I play dead, he'll leave me alone.

But he won't leave me alone. Instead, he continues the postmortem, and on top of it, he starts yelling. It's not intimidating, exactly, because Milton doesn't have the blustering roar of a man. He sounds more like a little boy throwing a tantrum in the supermarket checkout aisle. He keeps squealing, "What the f--- is *wrong* with you?"—not because I'm dead-drunk, but because I won't let him touch me.

I gain a little consciousness when I hear an empty rattling and realize Milton is punching the headboard with one fist. In the triangle of light that spills out of the bathroom, his eyes look like two thumbprints.

I squint to focus my gaze, while I try to concentrate on the power in my fingers. I feel like any woman in any movie that has, in order to save herself, willed her drugged or deadened digits to move. With enough meditative oomph, I finally complete the Jedi mind trick. My hand makes a swatting motion, and I hear a sloppy, smacking sound that says I've made contact. Milton rolls off the bed like a log, more because he's drunk than because of any real muscle on my part. I am finally left alone, permitted to curl back up with my drunkenness, hugging my own torso like a lover. From here on out, when anyone asks what happened, I'll say he's a brute, and he'll say I'm a prude.

For a few minutes in the early morning, I'll wake up prematurely and see Milton still sleeping on the floor where he fell, with the faded blue comforter wrapped around him like a torn fishing net. Sunlight will finger the room, and the bureau will be cluttered with cigarette butts and cigarette butt-filled bottles, and the carpet will hold the long, brown stain from somebody's rum and Coke. My lips will feel achy and swollen, and the sealed air will smell as musty as death.

I will decide I want to check out of all of this, maybe even for good.

CHAPTER 5

Current Perspectives on Underage Alcohol Policy

Underage Drinking Campaign Should Target Adults

National Research Council Institute of Medicine

In the following viewpoint, the Committee on Developing a Strategy to Reduce and Prevent Underage Drinking—formed by the National Research Council and the Institute of Medicine—proposes a national media campaign aimed at adults to address the underage drinking problem in the United States. Studies have shown that while most adults express concern about underage alcohol use, many grown-ups in fact contribute to underage drinking through sales to minors, purchasing alcohol for youths, or allowing youth parties where alcohol is served. The goal of a societal, adult-oriented media campaign, the committee maintains, is to convince parents and other adults that underage drinking happens on a large scale in their own communities and that they have a crucial role in the prevention and intervention of youth alcohol abuse.

The primary role of a societal, adult-oriented media campaign would be to convince parents and other adults not merely that there is a general problem with underage drinking in their communities, an idea that they appear to accept already, but also that it is very likely a problem for their own children and their children's friends, that there are important negative consequences of such alcohol use besides those risks associated with drinking and driving, and that they have an obligation to their children and the community to do something about it. The campaign would argue that by taking specific personal actions to prevent underage alcohol use, by increasing recommended parenting behaviors, and by support of community-level policies, parents and other adults can affect underage drinking and reduce its bad consequences.

The campaign rests on five assumptions:

- Many parents do not recognize either the prevalence of or the many risks associated with underage drinking for their own children.

- Many parents effectively facilitate their underage children's drinking by giving youth access to alcohol, by not responding to known incidents of children's drinking, and by not adequately monitoring and supervising their children's lives, generally.

- If parents changed their beliefs about the nature of underage alcohol use and its consequences, they would increase monitoring and other actions to limit their children's use.

- Because many underage drinkers obtain their alcohol from adult acquaintances or even strangers, if adults' willingness to buy alcohol for young people or to facilitate their drinking decreases, it would be more difficult for underage youths to obtain or use alcohol.

- If parents and other adults increased monitoring and other actions aiming to limit use, there would be a reduction in underage drinking, particularly heavy drinking.

What are the arguments in favor of such an adult-oriented campaign? One argument is that campaigns that offer new information are more promising than campaigns that revisit information that already has been widely distributed. Youth have often heard anti-alcohol messages addressed to them, but they have shown little change in recent years in most drinking behavior, although they have been somewhat responsive to the drinking and driving message. A new youth-focused campaign would be seen as old hat and redundant with what they are already hearing. In contrast, an adult-oriented campaign would present new messages. It would target parents and other adults, who are now facilitating youth alcohol use because they are not sufficiently aware of the problem for their children; not aware of the many harmful consequences of youth alcohol use; not aware that actions they take can affect the risks; and not aware that buying alcohol for underage persons or giving it to them, is socially irresponsible and usually illegal. For adults, in contrast with youth, there is the possibility of a communication program diffusing new information, which suggests greater effectiveness. In addition, it is possible that an adult-focused campaign may work to make what parents already believe more salient to them as they consider their actions to restrict their children's alcohol access. Effectively, a campaign can give them permission to act on the concerns they already have.

Disseminating Facts

An important question is what evidence is available that a large-scale communication campaign could affect awareness of extent and riskiness, and (assuming that such knowledge leads to motivation to act) teach effective actions.

There have been a small number of campaigns that tried to affect adult awareness of the extent and perceived riskiness of underage drinking and parental actions to reduce underage drinking, but they do not provide a solid foundation for estimating the promise for this approach. For example, the Australian National Alcohol Campaign in 2000 and 2001 primarily addressed youth, with some magazine advertising and brochure distribution to parents. However, the parent component was probably too small to expect much effect, and the evaluation information for parents does not provide an adequate basis for determining its behavioral effect. We then turn to less direct evidence that such a campaign will influence parent knowledge and behavior, relying on a reasonable

153

generalization of evidence from other programs. In some sense, it is possible to separate two aspects of such a campaign and ask about the availability of evidence for each.

Insofar as an adult-focused campaign is only presenting facts, not previously known by parents, there is good evidence that this can be accomplished readily. Diffusing facts is what communication programs do well.

There are many examples of diffusion of a new idea or set of facts through mass media. And there are some examples that suggest circumstances when simple diffusion of new facts was sufficient to produce behavior change. In one clear case, campaigns to encourage parents to put their infants to sleep on their backs to avoid sudden infant death syndrome have had fairly quick and widespread success. This behavior required a small change by parents and the changed sleeping position promised to avoid a dreaded consequence. Of most relevance for this discussion, the value of the back sleeping position represented new information for most parents.

Closer to the alcohol area, the idea of the "designated driver" diffused rapidly in the United States. The first mention of the term in the Lexis-Nexis electronic news major papers database is the fall of 1982, which is presumably when it was introduced to public discussion. By 1987, 91 percent of the respondents to a Gallup Poll indicated they approved of the idea. By 1988, the term could be used in questions without a parenthetical definition, suggesting that it was well known. The proportion of adults who reported using designated drivers also grew rapidly.

In terms of diffusing facts, the major issue is not whether it can be done, but whether a comprehensible and credible message can be transmitted with sufficient reach and frequency so that most people become aware of it and whether the particular facts encourage behavior change.

Changing Behavior?

The more difficult claim to support is not whether a mass media campaign can diffuse facts but whether it can effectively teach and, most important, influence specific new behaviors by adults. We do not know of any studies of a specific intervention of this sort relating to alcohol. The closest published example comes from Project Northland, which used only community-level media, along with other community activities, to try and affect parenting norms and behaviors. That limited intervention showed little effect on parental attitudes or behavior (although ... the initiative overall provides evidence for positive effects on youth). However, like the Australian campaign described above, Project Northland is a much more limited program than we propose, which would involve a national focus, heavy use of mass media, and involvement of the alcohol industry and other important institutions.

There is evidence that mass media campaigns, usually combining publicity and law enforcement, have succeeded in influencing drinking and driving. There is also evidence that campaigns have influenced the use of designated drivers.

Although there have been many campaigns to affect adult drinking behavior (other than driving), they have generally been understudied. For example, the National Institute on Alcohol Abuse and Alcoholism sponsored campaigns in 1971–1972, and in 1980–1982, and there is some published information about regular campaigns about drinking in Denmark from 1990 to 1996 and about single campaigns in other places. However the evaluations of those campaigns are weaker than those addressing drunk driving, and they often do not measure behavior or have credible comparison groups. In any case, these results, even the favorable ones about drunk driving, are not the same as evidence that parenting behaviors concerning their children's alcohol use can be affected. We recognize that in contrast to these other campaigns, the recommended campaign does not focus on a single behavior, nor does it focus on specific changes in adults' own behavior with regard to alcohol use. It urges parents and other adults to accept and act on a broad social norm, and it therefore has a longer time horizon than many of these more focused campaigns.

Although the available evidence bearing on the effectiveness of an adult-oriented campaign is modest, the committee is reasonably optimistic about the potential value of such a campaign, for two reasons. First, there is associational evidence that periods of broad national campaigns incorporating a variety of channels and institutional change efforts have been matched by periods of reductions in risky behavior. Those examples include the National High Blood Pressure Campaign from 1972 to 1984, the anti-tobacco efforts of the late 1960s–early 1970s, and the late 1990s–early 2000s, and the anti-drug campaigns of the middle 1980s.

Second, there is particularly strong evidence for the positive effects of media campaigns, which are able to link communication efforts with enforcement. The drinking and driving efforts described above were successful when they were able to link their messages to a specific expectation of enforcement. Similarly, seat belt use has climbed quickly when media publicity is linked to enforcement. Indeed one meta-analysis of the literature concludes that the largest effects evident in the mass media campaign literature come from campaigns which link media publicity with enforcement.

Underage Drinking Is Illegal, Not Just Irresponsible

Also pertinent to this aspect of the proposed campaign, both for parents and other adults, is the literature on compliance with the law. A central theme in the proposed campaign is that facilitating underage drinking is not only socially irresponsible but also illegal in most situations. Deterrence—through the threat of criminal prosecution or of civil liability for any injuries to third parties—can be part of the message, but the more powerful mechanism may be through the "expressive" or "declarative" function of the law, the mechanism through which the law registers social disapproval, teaches that the behavior is perhaps more dangerous than may have been appreciated, and thereby instills or reinforces the desired social norm. The mechanism here is not fear, but rather a powerful form of instruction drawing on the general desire to comply with legal rules.

This discussion has focused on intervening with parents and other adults in ways that encourage their active prevention of underage drinking specifically. However, there is a second route of intervention with parents that might well be incorporated into the proposed campaign. Evidence shows that the extent of supervision and monitoring by parents of youth, in general, affects youth initiation of risky behaviors and that intensive individual or group parent counseling can affect parenting behavior and, in turn, youth risk behaviors, including alcohol consumption. So a reasonable argument has been made that it would be worthwhile to attempt to communicate about new parenting behaviors, particularly through the use of advertising.

The Office of National Drug Control Policy (ONDCP) took this task on as a complement to its youth-focused campaign.... It dedicated nearly an equal amount of its ad campaign to parenting skills, particularly encouraging the close monitoring of children by parents. The expectation was that success in encouraging closer monitoring would in turn affect youth use of drugs. Thus far the evaluation of this component of the anti-drug campaign suggests mixed results. There is some evidence of an effect on the extent that parents talk with their children about drugs and for an effect on parental beliefs about the value of monitoring. The evidence for effects on actual monitoring and supervision is less strong, however. The ONDCP campaign is still ongoing, so definitive results are not yet available.

It may be possible that some actions to prevent youth drinking are easier to affect than general parent monitoring. For example, it may be easier to convince parents and other adults to stop facilitating drinking parties by their underage children than it is to encourage them to systematically monitor their children. Although this may be a sensible argument, there is not yet evidence to support it.

Colleges Explore Ways to Manage Binge Drinking on Campus

Jeffrey Kluger

In the following article, Jeffrey Kluger surveys some unconventional techniques that college administrators have advocated to reduce reckless drinking by students. Some officials have recommended a reduction in the legal drinking age from twenty-one to eighteen or nineteen so that colleges and universities can supervise and regulate student drinking on campus. Another approach, which many schools have actually implemented, has been to disseminate information around campus showing that moderation is practiced by the majority of students. In fact, the results of this technique on several college campuses show a significant reduction in high-risk drinking and lower instances of student delinquency. Still other administrators have urged the establishment of more early intervention programs and increased parental involvement to delay for as long as possible a child's first drink of alcohol, observing that kids who start drinking early are more likely to become binge drinkers as young adults.

The saga of the First Twins [Jenna and Barbara Bush] is fated to play on a while longer, now that Jenna Bush, 19, has decided to fight charges that she tried to buy liquor with someone else's ID at an Austin restaurant last month [in May 2001]. Caught with a margarita at the same haunt, her sister Barbara pleaded no contest last week [June 8, 2007] and will do eight hours of community service. While the President and his wife [George W. and Laura Bush] quietly grappled with how to manage their wayward children (it's Jenna's second citation), baby-boomer parents across the country had to

Jeffrey Kluger, "How to Manage Teen Drinking (The Smart Way)," *Time*, June 18, 2001. Reproduced by permission.

wonder: If the First Daughters could get into this kind of trouble with the press and public and even the Secret Service looking on, what might their own kids—living their lives outside such a bright circle of scrutiny—be up to? Chances are good that they're drinking too. Half the students age 10 to 24 questioned in a 1999 study by the Centers for Disease Control [and Prevention] said they had consumed alcohol in the preceding month. Boomer parents ought not to be too shocked. They whooped it up considerably more in their youths, according to National Institute on Alcohol Abuse and Alcoholism records that document how, across every age group, we've become an ever more sober society over the past two decades. In 1979, nearly 50% of 12- to 17-year-olds reported that they drank at some time in the previous month; now that figure is barely 20%. For kids 18 to 25, the stats fell from 75% to 60%. Still, the persistence of youthful drinking is forcing a new generation of parents to confront the dangers alcohol poses to their children and to contemplate the quandary of how to protect against the worst excesses.

College Officials Seek Ways to Diminish Binge Drinking

Often it is college administrators who have to deal directly with the most reckless imbibing. In studies through the 1990s by the Harvard School of Public Health, the percentage of college students who reported binge drinking within the previous two weeks remained steady at 44%. (Bingeing was defined as five drinks in a row for boys and four for girls.) In an age in which campus officials are increasingly seen as proxy parents, this is worrying to them. Legal liability is of particular concern, especially after M.I.T [Massachussetts Institute of Technology] ... [in 2000] chose to avoid a lawsuit by paying out $6 million to the parents of a freshman who in 1997 drank himself to death at a fraternity initiation.

One approach to reckless imbibing gaining currency among college administrators is unconventional and even counterintuitive. It argues for accepting that college-age kids are going to drink and for encouraging them to do so safely. Some campus officials recommend bowing to reality and lowering the drinking age, as 29 states did in the early '70s. By 1988, in response to the national mood against drunk driving and a threat by the Federal Government to cut off highway funding, every state had a minimum drinking age of 21. Researchers at the University of Michigan who studied the effects of the increase in the drinking age found that states on average reduced drinking among high school seniors 13.3%. The change also contributed to a 58% drop in alcohol-related auto deaths among 15- to 20-year-olds since 1982. A small chorus of university leaders believe, however, that the higher drinking age has in some ways made drinking more dangerous.

Reduced Drinking Age Might Lead to Better Regulation

When drinking is legal, they argue, it takes place in the open, where it can be supervised by police, security guards and even health-care workers. When the drinking age went up, the spigot wasn't turned off, it was simply moved underground—to homes or cars or frat-house basements—where no adult could keep an eye on things. When kids who are drinking on the sly do venture out, they often "pre-load" first, fueling up on as much alcohol as they can hold before the evening begins so that the buzz lasts as long as possible. As for the reduction in traffic fatalities? Skeptics believe it may have less to do with changing the drinking age than with the new mores about drunk driving and the more aggressive enforcement of DUI [driving under the influence] laws.

Doubtful about the value of the 21-year-old limit, administrators at Middlebury College in Vermont recently calculated how much federal highway money the state would lose were it to reduce the legal age to 18. Middlebury officials wanted to see if the school could afford to make up the difference. It couldn't (the figure was about $12.5 million last year), and the proposal died. But the idea didn't.

"The 21-year drinking age has not reduced drinking on campuses, it has probably increased it," says Middlebury president John McCardell. "Society expects us to graduate students who have been educated to drink responsibly. But society has severely circumscribed our ability to do that."

Other college administrators share McCardell's frustration. "If there were an 18- or 19-year-old drinking age, we could address the issues more favorably," says Dartmouth College President James Wright. As it is, "we can't go around sniffing students' breath or smelling their cups." Despite their complaints, college heads have been disinclined to make a public case for lowering the drinking age, knowing how controversial that would be. Meanwhile, on a number of campuses, administrators are employing what turns out to be a remarkably powerful tool to curb excessive drinking: simple information. When college students are asked how much drinking takes place on their campuses, they almost always guess too high. In a 1996 survey at Hobart and William Smith Colleges in New York, students said their peers were drinking five times a week. In truth, the answer was twice a week. In a different study, kids at 100 other campuses made similarly inflated estimates.

Simple Information Can Change Drinking Habits

Hobart and Smith sociology professor H. Wesley Perkins, who conducted the 1996 study, was intrigued by these findings. If teenagers—conformers by temperament—believe drinking is rampant on campus, might they be more inclined to pick up the habit? If on the other hand, they knew that the heavy drinkers were not in the majority, might moderation suddenly seem more attractive?

In 1997 Hobart and William Smith spent about $2,000 to find out. With the help of posters and newspaper ads, college officials publicized the fact that a majority of students on campus drank twice a week or less, that the majority of seniors consumed four or fewer drinks at parties, and that three-quarters of the alcohol on campus was consumed by just one-third of the students. The same messages popped up as screen savers on university computers.

Over the first two years, the university measured a 21% drop in high-risk drinking, which is imbibing five or more drinks in a sitting on a weekly basis. "That's a massive reduction when nationally those levels were flat or increasing slightly," says Perkins. The incidence of missed classes, unprotected sex, property damage and liquor-law violations also decreased.

The program, which has been dubbed the "social-norms" approach, is in effect at a number of other colleges—with similarly sparkling results. Northern Illinois University has seen a 44% reduction in binge drinking, Western Washington University is down 20% and the University of Missouri–Columbia is down 18%. One limitation to any college-based program is that many kids are arriving on campus with drinking problems. Fully half of binge drinkers do not wait for the freedom of college before they begin elbow bending in earnest; they start while they're still at home. "Colleges are inheriting behaviors learned in high school," says social psychologist Henry Weehsler, who heads Harvard's study on drinking among young people.

Parents Are Crucial to Delaying a Child's First Drink

Precollege drinking is especially worrisome given a central finding of recent alcohol research. Dr. Hoover Adger, professor and pediatrician at Johns Hopkins University in Baltimore, Md., has found that children who start drinking before age 15 are five times more likely to be alcohol dependent as adults. According to other studies, kids who start drinking early are also 10 times likelier to be involved in a fight after consuming alcohol, seven times likelier to be involved in a car accident and 12 times likelier to be injured. "Clearly, there is a huge benefit to delaying the first drink," says Adger.

But how on earth do you do that? Various surveys have shown that determined minors have a relatively easy time getting their hands on liquor, even if it's not kept in their own homes. They find adults who will buy it for them, or they use fake IDs, which today are widely available on the Internet.

Brenda Conlan and Jeffrey Wolfsberg, recovering alcoholics who founded Lifestyle Risk Reduction, which runs alcohol-education workshops for high schoolers and their parents, have made an informal study of nondrinkers and what keeps them sober. The most consistent nondrinkers, they've found, had unusually sound relationships with their parents, fearing less their discipline than the idea of disappointing them. "They have a relationship that means something to them," Conlan says.

Other researchers are confirming the primacy of the parent in keeping kids off alcohol. "If you look at two subsets," says Adger, "young people with good parental monitoring and those without, the difference in alcohol use is staggering." Among kids whose parents stay on top of their behavior, only about 10% drink at all, never mind drinking excessively, he says. That may seem an obvious finding. Still, it's reassuring to know that such a commonsense approach can yield such extraordinary results.

The Government Should Not Use Junk Science to Support Alcohol Policies

David Hanson and Matt Walcoff

David Hanson and Matt Walcoff assert that the federal government has improperly manipulated scientific data to support its position that raising the minimum drinking age to twenty-one has saved lives. The authors disparage the government's methodology as "junk science" that would never find support among impartial social scientists. Further, they contend, such a practice also undermines the federal bureaucracy's credibility about other important social issues, such as the need to wear seat belts or the dangerous health consequences of contracting HIV.

In July 2001 the U.S. Department of Justice [DOJ] announced an alleged breakthrough in research on alcohol policy. According to the DOJ, a comparison of drinking rates among American and European teenagers proved once and for all that Europe's more-liberal laws and attitudes regarding drinking by adolescents lead to greater alcohol problems.

Backers of the current U.S. drinking age—21, the world's highest—have adopted the DOJ's finding as if it were handed down from Mount Sinai. They refer to it whenever someone mentions that the rest of the world seems to do OK without making such a big deal out of drinking by young adults. The "fact" of European insobriety has been cited last year [2003] in letters to *The Journal of the American Medical Association* and *The Washington Post*. The Department of Education sent the second letter to an e-mail list of journalists who cover higher education.

David Hanson and Matt Walcoff, "Age of Propaganda," *Reason*, October 2004. Copyright 2004 by Reason Foundation, 3415 S. Sepulveda Blvd., Suite 400, Los Angeles, CA 90034, www.reason.com. Reproduced by permission.

Government Propagates Junk Science

Yet even a quick analysis of the DOJ's report finds that it does not stand up to scrutiny. The study never went through peer review, the process in which other researchers judge a study's merits before it gets published. The DOJ used outdated survey numbers even though newer ones were available, and its European figures left out several important countries, including France and Germany.

What's more, even the numbers the department did use do not back up the claims of those who tout its research. American teenagers had a higher rate of intoxication than their counterparts in half of the European countries. When compared to teenagers in Southern Europe, which has very liberal views regarding alcohol, American teens were more likely to have been drunk in the last 30 days (21 percent vs. 13 percent). And while more than half of the American teenagers who drank reported getting drunk, less than a fourth of young Southern European drinkers said they had been intoxicated.

It is hardly unknown for interest groups to tout such junk science; everyone remembers the claim that Super Bowl Sunday is the worst day of the year for domestic violence, or that abortion causes cancer. But when a government agency engages in such tactics, it gives the claim a false respectability. People tend to assume the government is an impartial arbiter, sorting through rival positions and conflicting data in an effort to arrive at the truth.

A Drinking Age Industry

Yet the federal bureaucracy has never served as a neutral moderator when it comes to alcohol policies. Rather than conduct reasoned, impartial scientific inquiry, agencies such as the DOJ, the Department of Transportation, and the National Institute on Alcohol Abuse and Alcoholism throw all their weight squarely on one side of the debate. Indeed, they have created a drinking age industry. Research designed to promote the current drinking age gets federal funding, a stamp of approval, and widespread dissemination, regardless of its scientific merit.

The oft-heard line that the increase in the drinking age from 18 to 21 has saved hundreds of lives per year is another good example. The Transportation Department claims it can estimate to the single digit how many people the law has saved: 927 in 2001, or nearly half the number of alcohol-related vehicular fatalities among 16–to–20-year-olds that year. No serious social scientist would ever make such an outlandish claim. Not only is it impossible to know what would have happened had the law not changed, but real research on the drinking age has not been able to verify a cause-and-effect relationship between the law and alcohol use or abuse. Many studies show no relationship between the two variables . . . others claim only that a few alcohol-related fatalities have shifted from the 18–21 age group to the 21–24 age group. . . . When it comes to the effects of the drinking age, the most you can say is that the jury is still out.

Yet the supposedly impartial federal bureaucracy still claims the drinking age has been as successful as the polio vaccine. An Internet search in the .gov domain finds more than 1,000 references to lives saved by the drinking age. It makes a great soundbite but poor public policy.

The bureaucracy's use of junk science is especially troubling because it calls into question the reliability of potentially life-saving information. If we cannot trust the government about the drinking age, some might argue, how can we trust it about the need to use seat belts, or the danger of HIV?

When it comes to alcohol policy, federal officials should stick to dispassionate, peer-reviewed research, not slick marketing aimed at promoting one point of view. They should act more like public servants and less like pressure groups.

Organizations to Contact

The editors have compiled the following list of organizations concerned with the issues debated in this book. The descriptions are derived from materials provided by the organizations. All have publications or information available for interested readers. The list was compiled on the date of publication of the present volume; the information provided here may change. Be aware that many organizations take several weeks or longer to respond to inquiries, so allow as much time as possible.

Al-Anon/Alateen

Al-Anon Family Groups Headquarters, Inc.
Virginia Beach, VA   23454-5617
(757) 563-1600 • fax: (757) 563-1655
e-mail: wso@al-anon.org
Web site: www.al-anon.alateen.org

Al-Anon/Alateen is a fellowship of men, women, and children whose lives have been affected by an alcoholic family member or friend. Alateen consists primarily of teenaged Al-Anon members who hold meetings in order to share experiences and learn how to deal with the effects of another person's drinking. Al-Anon/Alateen publications include several books, the monthly magazine the *Forum*, and the quarterly newsletter *Alateen Talk*.

Alcoholics Anonymous (AA)

A.A. World Services, Inc., PO Box 459
New York, NY   10163
(212) 870-3400
Web site: www.aa.org

Alcoholics Anonymous is a worldwide fellowship of sober alcoholics whose recovery is based on the Twelve Step program. AA requires no dues or fees and accepts no outside funds. It is self-supporting through voluntary contributions of members.

It is not affiliated with any other organization. AA's primary purpose is to carry the AA message to the alcoholic who still suffers. In addition to the *Alcoholics Anonymous Big Book,* the group's publications include the pamphlets *A Brief Guide to Alcoholics Anonymous* and *This Is A.A.: An Introduction to the A.A. Recovery Program,* and the quarterly newsletter *About AA.*

Alcohol: Problems and Solutions
c/o Prof. David J. Hanson, PhD, Potsdam, NY   13676
e-mail: hansondj@potsdam.edu
Web site: www2.potsdam.edu/hansondj/index.html

Alcohol: Problems and Solutions provides information on alcohol use and abuse and details effective ways to reduce or eliminate problems such as underage drinking, drinking and driving, and binge drinking. The Web site's "Alcohol and Youth" section includes articles on such topics as the minimum legal drinking age, effective and ineffective prevention methods associated with underage drinking, and the role that parents can play in educating their children about alcohol consumption.

The Beer Institute
122 C St. NW, Suite 350, Washington, DC   20001
(800) 379-BREW • fax: (202) 737-7004
e-mail: info@beerinstitute.org
Web site: www.beerinstitute.org

The Beer Institute is the official trade association for the American brewing industry. It promotes drinking in moderation and has implemented programs such as alcohol awareness curricula in schools and public service announcements to combat underage drinking and drunken driving. Its principal publication on this issue is *Signs of Progress: Declines in Underage Drinking and Drunk Driving.*

Center for Alcohol Marketing and Youth (CAMY)
Health Policy Institute, Georgetown University
Washington, DC   20057-1485

(202) 687-11019
e-mail: info@camy.org
Web site: camy.org

The Center for Alcohol Marketing and Youth (CAMY) at Georgetown University monitors the marketing practices of the alcohol industry to focus attention and action on industry practices that jeopardize the health and safety of America's youth. The center provides examples of how the marketing of alcoholic beverages can be appealing to youths, provides data on underage drinking to concerned individuals, and presents resources to those who want to take action to protect children from exposure to alcohol advertising. Publications include *Still Growing After All These Years: Youth Exposure to Alcohol Advertising on Television, 2001–2005. Underage Drinking in the United States: A Status Report, 2005,* and *Clicking with Kids: Alcohol Marketing and Youth on the Internet.*

Center for Science in the Public Interest (CSPI)—Alcohol Policies Project
1875 Connecticut Ave. NW, Suite 300
Washington, DC 20009-5728
(202) 332-9110 • fax: (202) 265-4954
Web site: www.cspinet.org/alcohol/index.html

The mission of the CSPI's Alcohol Policies Project is to reduce the devastating health and social consequences of drinking. The project's prevention-oriented policy strategy is aimed at curbing alcohol-related problems by advocating advertising reforms, increased excise taxes, and expanded warning requirements. Publications that focus on underage drinking in particular include *Preventing Youth Access to Alcohol from Commercial Sources, Adolescent Responses to Televised Beer Advertisements: Children of Alcoholics and Others,* and *Last Call for High-Risk Bar Promotions That Target College Students.*

Choose Responsibility
PO Box 507, Middlebury, VT 05753
(802) 398-2024 • fax: (802) 398-2029

e-mail: info@chooseresponsibility.org
Web site: www.chooseresponsibility.org

Choose Responsibility is a nonprofit organization committed to initiating an informed and open-mined public debate about the problem of reckless and excessive drinking in the United States, especially by young people. The group advocates rolling back the minimum legal drinking age from twenty-one to eighteen, implementing a comprehensive alcohol education program for young adults, and providing graduated alcohol licenses for eighteen- to twenty-year-olds. The organization's principal publication is a survey of the current minimum legal drinking age entitled *The Effects of the 21 Year-Old Drinking Age: A White Paper.*

College Alcohol Study (CAS)
Harvard School of Public Health, Boston, MA   02115
(617) 432-4388 • fax: (617) 432-3123
e-mail: hwechsle@hsph.harvard.edu
Web site: www.hsph.harvard.edu/cas

The Harvard School of Public Health College Alcohol Study (CAS) is an ongoing survey of over fourteen thousand students at 120 four-year colleges in forty states. The CAS focuses on college alcohol abuse, including the tradition of heavy drinking on college campuses; the role of alcohol in fraternities, sororities, and athletics; the relationship of state alcohol control measures and college policies to this behavior; and the role that easy access to alcohol and low prices play. Publications include the monograph *Binge Drinking on America's College Campuses: Findings from the Harvard School of Public Health College Alcohol Study* and a vast number of CAS studies and reports on numerous aspects of college alcohol consumption.

Distilled Spirits Council of the United States (DISCUS)
1250 Eye St. NW, Suite 400, Washington, DC   20005
(202) 628-3544
Web site: www.discus.org

The Distilled Spirits Council of the United States is the national trade association representing producers and marketers of distilled spirits sold in America. It seeks to ensure the responsible advertising and marketing of distilled spirits to adult consumers and to prevent such advertising and marketing from targeting individuals below the legal purchase age. The organization sponsors a number of public education programs designed to combat underage drinking and college binge drinking.

Higher Education Center for Alcohol and Other Drug Abuse and Violence Prevention
c/o Education Development Center, Inc., Newton, MA 02458
(800) 676-1730 • fax: (617) 928-1537
e-mail: HigherEdCtr@edc.org
Web site: www.higheredcenter.org

The Higher Education Center helps college and community leaders develop, implement, and evaluate programs and policies to reduce student problems related to alcohol and other drug use and interpersonal violence. The center promotes a combination of environmental management strategies to address the institutional, community, and public policy factors that contribute to these problems. In addition, the group supports the development of a prevention infrastructure, primarily by facilitating the work of statewide prevention initiatives and campus-community coalitions. The center publishes a quarterly newsletter entitled *Catalyst*.

Leadership to Keep Children Alcohol Free
c/o The CDM Group, Inc., Bethesda, MD 20814
(301) 654-6740 • fax: (301) 656-4012
e-mail: leadership@alcoholfreechildren.org
Web site: www.alcoholfreechildren.org

Leadership to Keep Children Alcohol Free is a coalition of governors' spouses, federal agencies, and public and private organizations committed to the prevention of alcohol use by children ages nine to fifteen. The goal of the coalition is to make childhood drinking prevention a national health priority. Its Web site provides statistics on underage drinking and its effects, as well as information on how individuals and organizations interested in this issue can take a leadership role in their community. Publications include *How Does Alcohol Affect the World of a Child? Keep Kids Alcohol Free: Strategies for Action*, and a newsletter entitled *Leadership Weekly Update*.

Mothers Against Drunk Driving (MADD)

MADD National Office, Irving, TX   75062
(800) 438-6233 • fax: (972) 869-2206
Web site: www.madd.org

Mothers Against Drunk Driving seeks to act as the voice of victims of drunk driving accidents by speaking on their behalf to communities, businesses, and educational groups and by providing materials for use in medical facilities and health and driver education programs. Its Web site's "Under 21" section features information for teens about alcohol and drunk driving. MADD publishes brochures such as *Underage Drinking: You Can Prevent It When They're Under Your Influence* and *Underage Drinking: You're Stronger than You Think*, the newsletter *MADDvocate*, and *Driven* magazine.

National Center on Addiction and Substance Abuse (CASA) at Columbia University

633 Third Ave., 19th Floor, New York, NY   10017-6706
(212) 841-5200 • fax: (212) 956-8020
Web site: www.casacolumbia.org

The National Center on Addiction and Substance Abuse (CASA) at Columbia University is a nonprofit organization whose goal is to inform Americans about the economic and social costs of substance abuse and its impact on their lives. CASA employs an interdisciplinary staff of more than sixty professionals with postgraduate and doctorate degrees, who have experience and expertise in various fields including substance abuse and addiction, communications, criminology, education, epidemiology, government, law, journalism, psychology, public administration, health and policy, social work, sociology and statistics. In addition to a quarterly newsletter, CASA's publications include the reports *Wasting the Best and the Brightest: Substance Abuse at America's Colleges and Universities, The Commercial Value of Underage and Pathological Drinking to the Alcohol Industry,* and *Teen Tipplers: America's Underage Drinking Epidemic.*

National Clearinghouse for Alcohol & Drug Information (NCADI)

PO Box 2345, Rockville, MD   20847-2345
(800) 729-6686 • fax: (240) 221-4292
e-mail: ncadi-info@samhsa.hhs.gov
Web site: ncadi.samhsa.gov

Managed by the Substance Abuse and Mental Health Services Administration (SAMHSA), the National Clearinghouse for Alcohol and Drug Information (NCADI) provides the most up-to-date and comprehensive information about substance abuse prevention and treatment in the United States NCADI offers more than 500 items to the public from various government agencies that produce materials related to substance abuse. The clearinghouse also employs information specialists who can recommend appropriate publications, posters, and videocassettes; conduct customized searches; provide grant and funding information; and refer people to appropriate organizations. Publications include *The Surgeon General's Call to Action to Prevent and Reduce Underage Drinking: A Guide to Action for Families, Binge Drinking and Youth: What Everyone Needs to Know,* and *Alcohol Alert No. 68: Young Adult Drinking.*

National Council on Alcoholism and Drug Dependence (NCADD)

244 East 58th St., 4th Floor, New York, NY   10022
(212) 269-7797 • fax: (212) 269-7510
e-mail: national@ncadd.org
Web site: www.ncadd.org

NCADD is a volunteer health organization that helps individuals overcome addictions, develops substance abuse prevention and education programs for youths, and advises the federal government on drug and alcohol policies. Publications include *What Should I Tell My Child About Drinking? Drinking Too Much Too Fast Can Kill You, Who's Got the Power? You . . . Or Drugs?* and *Girls! Straight Talk About Drinking and Drugs.*

National Institute on Alcohol Abuse and Alcoholism (NIAAA)

5635 Fishers Ln., MSC 9304, Bethesda, MD   20892-9304
(301) 443-3860
e-mail: niaaaweb-r@exchange.nih.gov
Web site: www.niaaa.nih.gov

NIAAA supports and conducts biomedical and behavioral research on the causes, consequences, treatment, and prevention of alcoholism and alcohol-related problems. Its College Drinking Initiative seeks to provide the NIAAA, policy makers, and college presidents with research on campus prevention, and treatment programs related to alcohol abuse. The agency publishes a quarterly, peer-reviewed scientific journal entitled *Alcohol Research & Health*, the *NIAAA Newsletter*, and *Alcohol Alert* bulletins, pamphlets, and reports.

Students Against Destructive Decisions (SADD)

SADD National, 255 Main St., Marlborough, MA   01752
(877) SADD-INC • fax (508) 481-5759
e-mail: info@sadd.org
Web site: www.saddonline.com

Also known as Students Against Drunk Driving, SADD's mission is to prevent underage drinking and drug use and to focus attention on the consequences of other decisions such as smoking, violence, and sexually transmitted diseases. SADD promotes an abstinence message for alcohol and other drugs and encourages students not to participate in activities with destructive consequences. The group publishes a newsletter, press releases, and also provides a "Contract for Life" that can be used to increase parent-child communication about alcohol and drug-related decisions.

The Wine Institute
425 Market St., Suite 1000, San Francisco, CA   94105
(415) 512-0151 • fax: (415) 442-0742
Web site: www.wineinstitute.org

The Wine Institute introduces and advocates public policy measures to enhance the environment for the responsible consumption and enjoyment of wine by adults. The organization endorses an Ad Code that promotes the healthy, moderate, and responsible consumption of wine among mature adults.

Bibliography

Books

Center on Alcohol Marketing and Youth — *Clicking with Kids: Alcohol Marketing and Youth on the Internet.* Washington, DC: Georgetown University, March 2004.

Centers for Disease Control and Prevention — *Life's First Great Crossroads: Tweens Make Choices That Affect Their Lives Forever.* Atlanta, GA: Centers for Disease Control and Prevention, 2000. www.cdc.gov/youthcampaign/research/PDF/LifesFirstCrossroads.pdf.

Committee on Education and the Workforce, U.S. House of Representatives — *Preventing Underage Drinking: What Works?* Washington DC: U.S. Government Printing Office, 2004.

Griffith Edwards — *Alcohol: The World's First Drug.* New York: St. Martin's, 2002.

Gary. L. Fisher — *Rethinking Our War on Drugs: Candid Talk About Controversial Issues.* Westport, CT: Praeger, 2006.

Marc Galanter, ed. — *Recent Developments in Alcoholism: Alcohol Problems in Adolescents and Young Adults.* 17. New York: Springer, 2005.

Carolyn Hilarski, ed. — *Addiction, Assessment, and Treatment with Adolescents, Adults, and Families.* Binghamton, NY: Haworth Social Work Practice, 2005.

Marjana Martinic and Barbara Leigh — *Reasonable Risk: Alcohol in Perspective.* New York: Brunner-Routledge, 2004.

Peter M. Monti, Suzanne M. Colby, and Tracy A. O'Leary, eds. — *Adolescents, Alcohol and Substance Abuse: Reaching Teens Through Brief Interventions.* New York: Guilford, 2001.

National Center on Addiction and Substance Abuse at Columbia University — *Wasting the Best and the Brightest: Substance Abuse at America's Colleges and Universities.* New York: National Center on Addiction and Substance Abuse at Columbia University, 2007.

James D. Orcutt and David R. Rudy, eds. — *Drugs, Alcohol, and Social Problems.* Lanham, MD: Rowman & Littlefield, 2003.

Gerry Stimson, Marcus Grant, Marie Choquet, and Preston Garrison — *Drinking in Context: Patterns, Interventions, and Partnerships.* New York: Routledge, 2007.

Substance Abuse and Mental Health Services Administration — *Results from the 2005 National Survey on Drug Use and Health: National Findings.* Rockville, MD: Office of Applied Studies, 2006.

Doug Thorburn — *Alcoholism Myths and Realities: Removing the Stigma of Society's Most Destructive Disease.* Northridge, CA: Galt, 2005.

U.S. Department of Health and Human Services	*The Surgeon General's Call to Action to Prevent and Reduce Underage Drinking 2007.* Rockville, MD: Office of the Surgeon General, 2007.
Stuart Walton	*Out of It: A Cultural History of Intoxication.* New York: Harmony, 2002.

Articles

ABC News	"Poll: Public Back Legal Drinking Age Limit: After 21 Years of Age-21 Drinking Public Support Remains Strong," May 22, 2005. http://abc news.go.com/Health/PollVault/ story?id=941810.
American Academy of Family Physicians	"Drinking: It Can Spin Your World Around: Facts for Teens," familydoc tor.org, September 2000.
American Medical Association	"Teenage Girls Targeted for Sweet-Flavored Alcoholic Beverages," Alco-holPolicyMD.com, January 4, 2006.
Sarah Baldauf	"Setting the Bar at 18," *U.S. News & World Report*, April 23, 2007.
Radley Balko	"Back to 18?" *Reason Magazine*, April 12, 2007.
Heather Baugham	"Surveys Say Teenage Binge Drinking a Problem," crescent-news.com, January 14, 2007. www.crescent-news .com/news/article/1479771.
Hope Cristol	"Teen Drinking Is on the Rise," *Futurist*, July–August 2002.

Thomas S. Dee and William N. Evans	"Teen Drinking and Educational Attainment: Evidence from Two-Sample Instructional Variables Estimates," *Journal of Labor Economics*, vol. 21, no. 1, 2003.
Randy Dotinga	"Teenage Alcoholism Can Have Lifelong Effects," *HealthDay News*, September 7, 2006. www.healthfinder.gov.
Gene Ford	"What About the Drinking Age? Why We Should Lower the Drinking Age to 19." Alcohol Problems and Solutions 2002. www2.postdam.edu/hansondj/YouthIssues/1046348192.html.
Wendy Cole Henderson	"Putting Limits on Teen Drivers," *Time*, October 15, 2006.
Miranda Hitti	"Teen Drinking, Drugs: Parents Unaware," *WebMD Medical News*, September 25, 2006. www.webmd.com/news/20060925/teen-drinking-drugs-parents-unaware.
John Kindelberger	"Calculating Lives Saved Due to Minimum Drinking Age Laws," National Highway Traffic Safety Administration: National Center for Statistics and Analysis, March 2005. http://www-nrd.nhtsa.dot.gov/pubs/809860.PDF.
Donna Leinwand	"Parents Warned About 24-Proof Gelatin," *USA Today*, July 3, 2002.

Karen MacPherson   "National Drinking Age of 21 Successful, Popular," *Pittsburgh Post-Gazette*, July 16, 2005.

Ben McFarland   "Calling Time on Drinks Promotions," *Incentive Today*, January 2005.

Jacqueline W. Miller, Timothy S. Naimi, Robert D. Brewer, and Sherry Everett Jones   "Binge Drinking and Associated Health Risk Behaviors Among High School Students," *Pediatrics*, vol. 119, no. 1, January 2007.

John J. Miller   "The Case Against 21," *National Review*, April 19, 2007.

National Center on Addiction and Substance Abuse at Columbia University   "The Commercial Value of Underage and Pathological Drinking to the Alcohol Industry," National Center on Addiction and Substance Abuse at Columbia University, May 2006. www.casacolumbia.org.

National Highway Traffic Safety Administration   "Young Drivers," National Highway Traffic Administration: National Center for Statistic and Analysis, 2005. http://www-nrd.nhtsa.dot.gov/Pubs/809774.PDF.

National Institute on Alcohol Abuse and Alcoholism   "Early Drinking Linked to Higher Lifetime Alcoholism Risk," *NIH News*, July 3, 2006. www.nih/gov/news/pr/jul2006/niaaa-03.htm.

National Institute on Alcohol Abuse and Alcoholism | "Underage Drinking: A Major Public Health Challenge" (Alcohol Alert No. 59), National Institute on Alcohol Abuse and Alcoholism, April 2003. http://pubs.niaaa.nih.gov/publications/aa59.htm.

National Institute on Alcohol Abuse and Alcoholism | "Young Adult Drinking" (Alcohol Alert No. 68), National Institute on Alcohol Abuse and Alcoholism, April 2006. http://pubs.niaaa.nih.gov/publications/aa68/aa68.htm.

National Survey on Drug Use and Health | "Alcohol Use and Delinquent Behaviors Among Youths," *The NSDUH Report*, April 1, 2005. www.oas.samhsa.gov/2k-5/alcDelinquent/alcDelinquent.htm.

Jon P. Nelson | "Advertising, Alcohol, and Youth," *Regulation*, Summer 2005.

Amy Norton | "Teen Binge Drinking Can Do Long-Term Brain Damage," rense.com, February 14, 2005. www.rense.com/general63/dolon.htm.

Office of Juvenille Justice and Delinquency Prevention | "Youth Drinking Rates and Problems: A Comparison of European Countries and the United States," Office of Juvenile Justice and Delinquency Prevention, May 2005.

David K. Rehr   "Q: Are New Congressional Efforts to Curb Teenage Drinking on the Right Track? NO: Let's Focus on Real Solutions to Fight Underage Drinking," *Insight on the News*, October 27, 2003.

Andrea Sattinger,   "The *Teen People* Drinking Poll," *Teen*
Mark J. Miller,   *People*, vol #8, no. 5, June 1, 2005.
and Ansley Roan

Susan   "Dying for a Drink," *People*, vol. 66,
Schindehette and   no. 10, September 4, 2006.
Ken Lee

Paula Wasley   "A Former College President Starts a National Campaign to Lower the Drinking Age," *Chronicle of Higher Education*, April 6, 2007.

George F. Will   "Drinking Age Paradox," *Washington Post*, April 19, 2007.

Women's Health   "Girls More Likely Than Boys to Be
Weekly   Overexposed to Alcohol Ads in Magazines," July 29, 2004.

Index